BASIC IDEAS OF
MONTESSORI'S EDUCATIONAL
THEORY

Photograph: Jack Esten – Archive of the Association Montessori Internationale 161, Koninginneweg, NL-1075 CN Amsterdam.

THE CLIO MONTESSORI SERIES
VOLUME 14

BASIC IDEAS OF MONTESSORI'S EDUCATIONAL THEORY:
Extracts from Maria Montessori's Writings and Teachings

Maria Montessori

Originally compiled by Paul Oswald and
Günter Schulz-Benesch

Translated from the German by
Lawrence Salmon

CLIO PRESS
OXFORD, ENGLAND

This edition has been licensed for publication by the Association
Montessori Internationale, Amsterdam. *Basic Ideas of Montessori's
Educational Theory* was first published in German in 1967 under the
title *Grundgedanken der Montessori-Pädagogik* (Freiburg im
Breisgau: Verlag Herder) and was originally compiled from Maria
Montessori's writings and teachings by Paul Oswald and Günter
Schulz-Benesch. The German publication is now in its fifteenth
edition (1997).

British Library Cataloguing in Publication Data

Montessori, Maria 1870–1952
  Basic ideas of Montessori's educational theory. – (Clio
  Montessori series ; v. 14)
  1. Montessori method of education
  I. Title II. Oswald, Paul III. Schulz-Benesch, Günter
  371.3'92
ISBN 1–85109–276–5

ABC-Clio Ltd.,
26 Beaumont Street,
OXFORD OX1 2NP, ENGLAND

Cover design and typesetting by Columns Design Ltd.,
Reading, England
Printed and bound in Great Britain by
Halstan & Co., Ltd. Amersham, Buckinghamshire

CONTENTS

Foreword to the English Edition   vii

I. The Forgotten Fellow Citizen   1

    The Child in Modern Society   1

II. Children are Different   10

    The Discovery of the Spirit (The Polarization of Attention)   10

III. Keys to the World   19

    A. A New Education: "The Foundations of my Pedagogy"   19

    B. Key Concepts of Montessori's Pedagogy   39

      1. "Milk and Love": The "Psychic Embryo"   39

      2. The Child and the World: The "Absorbent Mind" and the "Sensitive Periods"   58

      3. Freedom and Commitment: The "Prepared Environment"   67

      4. The Individual and the Community: "Wasted Energies"?   89

      5. Good and Evil: The New Educator and the Child's Conscience   100

      6. Education and Peace: "The Single Nation"   113

      7. Man and the World: "Cosmic Education"   128

CONTENTS

C. Practical Texts   133

  1. The Children's House

    Helene Helming, Our Children's House   133

  2. The Montessori School

    Hans Elsner: Everyone has the right to

    be himself   139

  3. The Montessori Grammar School

    Maria Montessori, her ideas for a

    secondary school   151

    H.-J. Jordan, What is a Montessori

    secondary school?   154

  4. A Sequel: Montessori in the Area of Special

    Education

    Karl Neise, Montessori and Remedial

    Education   162

    Theodor Hellbrügge, The discovery of

    the relevance of Montessori's educational

    theory to handicapped children   168

IV. The Secret Centre   177

  God and the Child   177

V. The Adventure of a Life in the Service of the

  Child (by G. Schulz-Benesch)   187

Bibliographical Appendix   205

FOREWORD TO THE ENGLISH EDITION

Prof. Dr. Schulz-Benesch

The publication of this compilation of the "Basic Ideas of Montessori's Educational Theory" was initially motivated by the fact that Montessori's writings are scattered throughout her long lifetime, and are extant in several languages. Montessori's ideas and educational practice were inaccessible in many places, and a compilation of authentic passages aimed to make her work readily available. Since then, reprints of Montessori's earlier books have appeared in German, and now also in English, along with previously unpublished works from the Montessori legacy,[1] meeting the demand for greater reading matter.

The many reprints of this volume, however, are to be seen in the light of the *main reason* for its publication, which remains as before: the range of Montessori's output and a certain lack of order in her writings (many of which actually originated as lecture notes) suggest the need to allow the author herself *to summarize* her basic ideas on education in this limited space – *an introduction to Montessori by Montessori*, as it were.

Continuing international demand prompted us to make the thought and work of the great educationalist more readily accessible in this way, not only to readers with a special interest in Montessori, but to all those who are concerned with educational issues. Real-life illustration is provided by the reports by various authors dealing with practical work and the further development of Montessori's theory in the field of special education. The volume ends with a brief biography of this important Italian woman and cosmopolitan figure.

---

[1] cf. M. Montessori, The Child, Society and the World, Oxford 1989.

FOREWORD TO THE ENGLISH EDITION

We share the belief of the Nobel Prize winner Nico Tinbergen "that by 'decoding' Montessori's slightly Victorian language and rephrasing it in modern idiom, one recognises her unique genius, and we are convinced that her ideas deserve as close study as those of Darwin and Freud".[2] Indeed, we would add that Montessori's continuing relevance has its roots in her shrewd observation of the phenomena of child behaviour and *at the same time* in her understanding of the universal human significance of education: "... today education is not so much interested in science as in humanity and civilization, which has only one fatherland, the world". Thus wrote Montessori as early as 1909 in her first famous book.[3]

---

[2] E. A. Tinbergen//N. Tinbergen, Early Childhood Autism – An Ethological Approach, in: Zeitschrift für Tierpsychologie, supplement 10 (1972), p. 52
[3] M. Montessori, The Discovery of the Child, Oxford 1988, p. 5

I

THE FORGOTTEN FELLOW CITIZEN

The Child in Modern Society

1938 (1) The child, who is the essence of a natural being, lives, on the face of it, alongside the adult, and depending on the parental home is subject to the most varied conditions. However, he will always remain alien to the social labour of the adult, for the social production process has no use for the child's activity. Indeed, we must bear in mind that the child has absolutely no possibility of sharing in the social labour of the adult. If we take as a symbol of manual labour that of a blacksmith pounding a massive anvil with his hammer, then we realize that the child would never be capable of such an effort. If on the other hand we envisage as a symbol of intellectual labour that of a scientist carrying out complicated research with the aid of highly sensitive instruments, we recognize that in this area also the child cannot be expected to contribute. And, finally, if we think of a legal expert striving to improve the law, then we shall be left in no doubt that his place as well cannot be taken by the child.

The child is entirely alien to this society of men, and his position might be characterized by the words of the Bible "My Kingdom is not of this world". He is therefore a being who lives entirely apart from the social order created by men, a stranger in the artificial world which man has constructed for himself alongside and away from nature. In the world into which he is born, the child is first and foremost an extra-social being, if by that we understand someone who is not able to adapt to human society, nor to take part in its productive labours or the rules of its organization, and who thus disturbs the established order. In fact, in all adult

1

society the child is an outsider who invariably has a disruptive influence, even in his own home. His inability to adapt is aggravated by the fact that he is an active being, and unable to live without activity. Hence the need to oppose this activity, to force the child to restrain himself and not to cause any annoyance, to reduce him to passivity. So he is shut up in special rooms called playrooms and nurseries which, though not prisons like those provided for certain types of antisocial adult, are nevertheless something fairly similar. Or else he is banished to school, to that exile which adults reserve for children until they are able to live in the adult world without disrupting it. Only then can he be admitted to human society. First he must submit to the adult like someone with no civil rights, since from a social perspective he does not even exist. The adult is his lord and master, and the child remains subject to his orders, from which there is no appeal, and which are consequently considered a priori just. The small child appears from nowhere on the family scene, and the adult to him is big and powerful like a god, and is the only one who can provide for his vital needs. The adult is his creator, his providence, his master, his judge. Never has anyone been so completely and utterly dependent on another as the child is on the adult.

1938 (2) Parents must openly and willingly confront the most burning social issue: the struggle for the recognition of the rights of the child.

Much has been said in recent years about the rights of man, and especially about the rights of the worker. But now the time has come when we must speak of the social rights of the child. The labour question lays the foundations for social change, but mankind lives solely from human labour, and so the material existence of humanity as a whole was dependent on the solution to the problem. But if the labourer produces what man consumes – and is a creator of external objects – the child produces nothing less than mankind itself, and for that reason concern for his rights makes social transformation all the more urgent. It is unnecessary to point out

2

that society should provide children with the fullest and most judicious care – for they after all are the ones from whom we hope for greater strength and greater opportunities for the people of tomorrow.

The fact that the rights of the child have been forgotten and ignored, that the child has been mistreated, even destroyed, and that moreover his worth, power and nature have been misunderstood, should all give humanity serious food for thought.

1949 (3) The field of child-life and child-education is one in which all have had experience right from the beginning of man's appearance on earth, and in which they continue to have experience. These experiences have had a long time to consolidate and to become universal. Unfortunately there are also modern branches of science or attempts at science, which have developed around the most superficial manifestations of child behaviour (actually around the "effects" of outer circumstances) and these reached an easy compromise with those prejudices which every adult cherishes regarding the child. That is why the manifestations of child-life which we mentioned are not observed by people "who have eyes and see" but by those already blinded by prejudice.

These prejudices are so universal that it is difficult to have them recognized as such. They are confused and strengthened by the evidence of facts because all, or nearly all, see the child as he is commonly recognized, not the child as he is, still an unknown entity. In fact if one should tell an audience that in order to reform education many prejudices have to be overcome, the most progressive and unbiased among the listeners would think at once of prejudices relating to what has, or has not, to be taught and not of prejudices regarding the child himself. They think that it is a question of removing prejudices and errors from what is taught, so as not to transmit them to the younger generation. Some hold that the teaching of dogmatic religious conceptions should be avoided; others that teaching must abolish prejudice between the social classes; others again that certain formal habits no

3

longer belonging to our society should be eliminated, and so on.

It seems, however, as yet inconceivable that there are prejudices which "prevent" us from seeing the child from a point of view different from that which is usually taken of him.

Yet those who study child-psychology and education must take into account, not those social prejudices which bother modern educationalists so much, but *other* prejudices – those which concern the child *directly*, his natural attributes and powers, the abnormal conditions of his life.

By removing religious prejudice, it may perhaps be possible to understand better the greatness or significance of religions but not the natural personality of the child. By removing prejudices concerning social castes, it may be possible to intensify the understanding and harmony between the members of society, but it will not help to a better understanding of the child. If many formalities in our social relations are recognized to be futile, belonging to the past, we may witness a reform of social customs, but we will not understand the child any better.

All that seems to contribute to social progress among adults can, according to common opinion, leave the vital necessities of childhood aside. The adult has always seen only himself in society and in its progress. The child has remained outside society – an unknown quantity in the equation of life.

Hence a prejudice has found its way into the adult – the notion that the life of the child can be changed or improved only through teaching. This prejudice impedes the understanding of the fact that the child constructs himself, that he has a *teacher* within himself and that this inner teacher also follows a programme and a technique of education, and that we adults by acknowledging this unknown teacher may enjoy the privilege and good fortune of becoming its assistants and faithful servants by helping it with our co-operation.

Many other prejudices are the logical consequences of this one. It is said that the mind of a child is empty – without a

4

guide and without laws of its own. Adults, therefore, are supposed to have the great and complete responsibility of filling it, guiding and commanding it. It is believed that the child is naturally inclined towards a number of defects, towards decadence and inertia, that by nature it is blown hither and thither as a feather driven before the wind, and that adults, therefore, must stimulate and encourage him, correct and guide him all the time.

In the same way it is assumed in the physical order that the child cannot control his movements and is incapable of taking care of himself, and so the adult hurries to do everything for him without bothering to consider what the child can very well manage alone. The child is then said to be a heavy burden and a great responsibility as he requires this constant care. The attitude of the adult to the child is that he must "create" in him a grown-up man and that the intelligence, the socially useful activity, the character of this human being, who has entered his home, are all his work.

Then pride is born as an accompaniment to this anxiety and sense of responsibility. The child seen in this light owes infinite respect and gratitude to his creators, his saviours. If, instead, he rebels he must be corrected, must be brought into submission with the help of violence, if necessary. In order to be perfect, the child must then be perfectly passive and most rigorously obedient. He is a perfect parasite of his parents and as long as these assume the whole economical burden of his life, he must depend upon them absolutely. He is a "child". Even when he has grown up and has to shave regularly each morning before attending the University, he still remains dependent upon his father and teachers just as when he was still a child. He must go where his father wishes him to go, study, often, as his teachers and professors wish him to study. He will remain outside society even when he takes his degree and may be 26 years of age ...

... The personality of the child has remained buried under the prejudices of order and justice. Though the adult has agitated very strongly in defence of his own rights, he has overlooked those of the child. He is not even aware of him.

On this plane, life has continued to evolve and to complicate itself up to the present century.

From the complex whole of such conceptions arise the particular prejudices which impose themselves under the cloak of so praiseworthy an aim as the protection of, and respect for, the life of childhood.

The small child, for example, should not be let to do any form of *work*. He must be abandoned to a life of intellectual inertia. He should only play in a certain well-established way.

If, therefore, one day it is discovered that the child is a great worker, who can apply himself to his work with concentration, who can learn by himself, teach himself and who possesses discipline within himself, this seems to be like a fairy tale. It does not evoke surprise, it just appears utterly absurd.

No attention is paid to this *reality*, and hence no conclusion is reached to the effect that in this apparent contradiction may be hidden an *error* on the part of the adult. It is simply impossible, it cannot exist – or as it is said, it is not serious.

The greatest difficulty in the way of an attempt to give freedom to the child and to bring its powers to light does not lie in finding a form of education which realizes these aims. It lies rather in overcoming the prejudices which the adult has formed in his regard. That is why I said we must recognize, investigate and fight against "the prejudices concerning the child" only, without touching other prejudices which the adult may have formed regarding his own life.

This struggle against prejudices is the social question of the child which must accompany the renewal of its education. It is, in other words, imperative to prepare a positive and well-defined *route* leading to this goal. If the prejudices concerning the child are directly and *exclusively* aimed at, a *reform of the adult* will accompany it step by step because an obstacle in the adult will have been removed. This reform of the adult is of enormous importance for society as a whole. It represents the reawakening of a part of human consciousness which has been covering itself progressively with layer upon layer of impediments. Moreover, without this awakening, all other social questions become obscure and the problems raised by them insoluble. "Consciousness" has been dimmed, not in some adults only, but in all adults – because all have dealings with children. As their consciousness is dimmed regarding the child, so they also act unconsciously. On this point they do not use their powers of reflexion, their intelligence which leads them to make progress in other fields. There is in them, as we already mentioned, a *blind spot*, similar to that on the retina of the eye. The child, that unknown being, that only apparently human being, sometimes considered almost as a matrimonial accident, who opens a road of sacrifices and duties, does not in himself arouse either awe or admiration.

Let me describe a psychological complex. Suppose that in nature the child appeared to be a divine miracle, of the sort men feel in the presence of the image of the Child Jesus, which inspires artists and poets and represents the hope of redemption for all mankind, an august figure at whose feet the kings of the East and West devoutly place their gifts. The child Jesus is also, however, amid the religious worship paid to Him, a real child, a newly-born babe without consciousness. Almost all parents feel similar lofty sentiments at the birth of their child, who is idealized by the strength of their love. Later, however, as this child grows up, he begins to be a nuisance. Almost remorsefully they begin to defend themselves against him. They are happy when he is asleep and try to make him sleep as long as possible. Those who can, hand their child over to the care of a nurse and, taking courage, instruct her to keep him away from them as much as possible. If this unknown and incomprehensible being, acting in obedience to unconscious urges, does not submit, he is punished, fought against, and being weak and defenceless both intellectually and physically, he must bear all. In the adult's soul there occurs a "conflict" because he does love the child. At first this conflict causes pain and remorse. Later, however, the psychic mechanism at play between the conscious and the subconscious in man reaches a form of adaptation. As

Freud would say, there occurs a fugue. The subconscious prevails, i.e. it suggests, "What you do is not in order to defend yourself against the child, it is a duty you perform in his regard. It is a necessary good. You must even act bravely because you are 'educating' the child. You are striving to build up goodness in him". When this comfort is obtained, the natural feelings of admiration and love are effectively buried ...

1946 (4) It must be that there is something lacking in the treatment of children everywhere and of every age. We must take a new element into consideration. Perhaps man's behaviour has changed in this complicated world, perhaps he disregards something fundamental and family life is different and the children are the first victims of this disregard. We must consider children from this point of view. Moral and social education are so closely related that we must have some new contribution for moral hygiene. It is evident that these children suffer. It is evident too that modern psychology is not sufficient. All the things we have had up to date for moral education have not been enough. The facts prove it. The question of moral education is not as simple as it was before. Some other element must be added to correlate with the present form of society which is different from what it was formerly. Moral and mental hygiene especially must be developed in order to protect children. The relationship between the family, the teacher and the children must be harmonious because the school environment plays a larger part than it did before. Both the teacher and the parents must have the help of psychic knowledge that was not known before ...

Goodwill alone is not enough. Today we need a positive contribution towards the betterment of the human soul. There must be a mental and moral hygiene towards which family, school and city all make a contribution. This will be the progress of civilization.

The progress and the growth of the individual are very important. Progress is the care of the psyche of the individual in relationship to the environment. It is not a question of doing something for the individual first and then something for society, for it is in society that the root lies. We must see the individual in his place in society because no individual can develop without the influence of society …

Sources: (1) *Kinder sind anders*, p. 267–268; (2) *Ibid*, p. 290–291; (3) *The Formation of Man*, p. 44–50; (4) *The Child, Society and the World*, p. 74–75.

II

CHILDREN ARE DIFFERENT

The Discovery of the Spirit (The Polarization of Attention)

1916 (1) **The organization of psychical life begins with the characteristic phenomenon of attention.**

My experimental work with little children from three to six years old has been, in fact, a practical contribution to research which has for its aim the discovery of the treatment required by the soul of the child, a treatment analogous to that which hygiene prescribes for its body.

I think, therefore, that it is essential to record the fundamental fact which led me to define my method.

I was making my first essays in applying the principles and part of the material I had used for many years previously in the education of deficient children, to the normal children of the San Lorenzo quarter in Rome, when I happened to notice a little girl of about three years old deeply absorbed in a set of solid insets, removing the wooden cylinders from their respective holes and replacing them. The expression on the child's face was one of such concentrated attention that it seemed to me an extraordinary manifestation; up to this time none of the children had ever shown such fixity of interest in an object; and my belief in the characteristic instability of attention in young children, who flit incessantly from one thing to another, made me peculiarly alive to the phenomenon.

I watched the child intently without disturbing her at first, and began to count how many times she repeated the exercise; then, seeing that she was continuing for a long time, I picked up the little arm-chair in which she was seated, and

10

placed chair and child upon the table; the little creature hastily caught up her case of insets, laid it across the arms of her chair, and gathering the cylinders into her lap, set to work again. Then I called upon all the children to sing; they sang, but the little girl continued undisturbed, repeating her exercise even after the short song had come to an end. I counted forty-four repetitions; when at last she ceased, it was quite independently of any surrounding stimuli which might have distracted her, and she looked round with a satisfied air, almost as if awaking from a refreshing nap.

I think my never-to-be-forgotten impression was that experienced by one who has made a discovery.

This phenomenon gradually became common among the children: it may therefore be recorded as a constant reaction occurring in connection with certain external conditions, which may be determined. And each time that such a polarization of attention took place, the child began to be completely transformed, to become calmer, more intelligent, and more expansive; it showed extraordinary spiritual qualities, recalling the phenomena of a higher consciousness, such as those of conversion.

It was as if in a saturated solution, a point of crystallization had formed, round which the whole chaotic and fluctuating mass united, producing a crystal of wonderful forms. Thus, when the phenomenon of the polarization of attention had taken place, all that was disorderly and fluctuating in the consciousness of the child seemed to be organizing itself into a spiritual creation, the surprising characteristics of which are reproduced in every individual.

It made one think of the *life of man* which may remain diffused among a multiplicity of things, in an inferior state of chaos, until some special thing attracts it intensely and fixes it; and then man is revealed unto himself, he feels that he has begun to live.

This spiritual phenomenon which may co-involve the entire consciousness of the adult, is therefore only one of the constant elements of the phenomena of "internal formation". It occurs as the normal beginning of the inner life of children, and accompanies its development in such a manner as to become accessible to research, as an experimental fact.

It was thus that the soul of the child gave its revelations, and under their guidance a method exemplifying spiritual liberty was evolved.

The story of this initiatory episode soon spread throughout the world, and at first it seemed like the story of a miracle. Then by degrees, as experiments were made among the most diverse races, the simple and evident principles of this spiritual "treatment" were manifested.

Psychical development is organized by the aid of external stimuli, which may be determined experimentally.

The contribution I have made to the education of young children tends, in fact, to *specify* by means of the revelations due to experiment, the form of liberty in internal development.

It would not be possible to conceive liberty of development, if by its very nature the child were not capable of a spontaneous organic development, if the tendency to develop his energies (expansion of latent powers), the conquest of the means necessary to a harmonious innate development, did not already exist. In order to expand, the child, left at liberty to exercise his activities, ought to find in his surroundings something *organized* in direct relation to his internal organization which is developing itself by natural laws, just as the free insect finds in the form and qualities of flowers a direct correspondence between form and sustenance. The insect is undoubtedly free when, seeking the nectar which nourishes it, it is in reality helping the reproduction of the plant. There is nothing more marvellous in Nature than the correspondence between the organs of these two orders of beings destined to such a providential co-operation.

The secret of the free development of the child consists, therefore, in organizing for him the means necessary for his internal nourishment, means corresponding to a primitive impulse of the child, comparable to that which makes the new-born infant capable of sucking milk from the breast, which by its external form and elaborated sustenance, corresponds perfectly to the requirements of the infant.

It is in the satisfaction of this primitive impulse, this internal hunger, that the child's personality begins to organize itself and reveal its characteristics; just as the new-born infant, in nourishing itself, organizes its body and its natural movements.

We must not therefore set ourselves the educational problem of seeking means whereby to organize the internal personality of the child and develop his characteristics; the sole problem is that of offering the child the necessary nourishment.

It is by this means that the child develops an organized and complex activity which, while it responds to a primitive impulse, exercises the intelligence and develops qualities we consider lofty, and which we supposed were foreign to the nature of the young child, such as patience and perseverance in work, and in the moral order, obedience, gentleness, affection, politeness, serenity; qualities we are accustomed to divide into different categories, and as to which, hitherto, we have cherished the illusion that it was our task to develop them gradually by our direct interposition, although in practice we have never known by what means to do so successfully.

In order that the phenomenon should come to pass it is *necessary* that the spontaneous development of the child should be accorded *perfect liberty*; that is to say, that its calm and peaceful expansion should not be disturbed by the intervention of an untimely and disturbing influence; just as the body of the new-born infant should be left in peace to assimilate its nourishment and grow properly.

In such an attitude ought we to await the *miracles* of the inner life, its expansions and also its unforeseen and surprising explosions; just as the intelligent mother, only giving her baby nourishment and rest, contemplates it seeing it *grow*, and awaits the manifestations of nature: the first

13

tooth, the first word, and finally the action by which the baby will one day rise to his feet and walk.

But to ensure the psychical phenomena of growth, we must prepare the "environment" in a definite manner, and from this environment offer the child the external means directly necessary for him.

This is the *positive* fact which my experiment has rendered concrete. Hitherto the liberty of the child has been vaguely discussed; no clearly defined limit has been established between liberty and abandonment. We were told: "Liberty has its limits", "Liberty must be properly understood". But a special method indicating "how liberty should be interpreted, and what is the intuitive *quid* which ought to co-exist with it", has not been determined.

The establishment of such a method should open up a new path to all education.

1923 (2) ... If the child found his area of activity correspondent to his inner needs, he would reveal to us even more that is necessary for his development. He seeks rapport with the type of human beings who surround him, and he finds it.

But there are individual inner needs, for which, while the child has buried himself in his own special work, there must be complete solitude and a separation from everything and everyone. No one can help us to achieve the intimate isolation by which we find our secret worlds, so mysterious, rich and full. If others intervene, it is destroyed. This degree of thought, which we attain by freeing ourselves from the external world, must be fed by the inner spirit, and our surroundings cannot influence us in any way other than to leave us in peace.

Great, or exceptional men exhibit the ability to achieve this degree of profound thought, and it is their source of inner strength. There are great men who, from this power of thought, have derived the faculty of influencing masses of people with a quiet thoughtfulness and infinite benevolence. There are men who, after a prolonged absence from the world of affairs, feel obliged to resolve the great problems of mankind while with infinite patience they support the weaknesses and imperfections of their peers, who have themselves succumbed to hatred and aggression. Furthermore, we see that there exists a strict relationship between manual labour and deep concentration of the spirit. At first glance these might appear to be opposed, but they are profoundly compatible, for the one is the source of the other. The life of the spirit prepares the dynamic power for daily life, and, on its side, daily life encourages thought by means of ordinary work. The physical energy expended is continually renewed through the spirit, giving rise to a continual interrelationship. The man who understands himself clearly responds to the necessities of his inner life exactly as the body responds to physical necessities such as hunger and sleep. The mind that does not respond to its own spiritual necessities runs the same risks as the body that no longer responds to hunger pangs or the need to rest.

But because we find in children this power of thought, this immersion of the spirit within itself, it is clear that this quality is not peculiar to exceptional or particularly gifted people, but is a universal human trait preserved in only a few people in their maturity.

If we consider these flickering powers of concentration in children, we must move to a different area than that considered in the discussion of useful work. An object that is not in the least useful will attract the immediate attention of a child. He will occupy himself with it and manipulate it in every possible way. Often his manipulations will not be very orderly; often he will destroy what he began the moment before and will have to begin at the beginning again. These movements will be repeated so many times that the task does not appear to be performed with particular enthusiasm, but we are viewing a special phenomenon …

… When the children had completed an absorbing bit of work, they appeared rested and deeply pleased. It almost seemed as if a road had opened up within their souls that led to all their latent powers, revealing the better part of themselves. They exhibited a great affability to everyone, put themselves out to help others and seemed full of good will. Then it would happen that one of them would quietly approach the teacher and whisper to her, as if confiding a great secret, "I'm a good boy!".

This observation has already been found valuable by others, but it is particularly useful to me. I took what happened within the children to be a law, and this made it possible for me to resolve completely the problem of education. It was clear to me that the concept of order and the development of character, of the intellectual and emotional life, must derive from this veiled source. Thereafter, I set out to find experimental objects that would make this concentration possible, and carefully worked out an environment that would present the most favourable external conditions for this concentration. And that is how my method began.

Certainly here lies the key to all pedagogy: to learn to recognize precious moments of concentration ...

1946 (3) When we speak about freedom in education we mean freedom for the creative energy which is the urge of life towards the development of the individual. This is not a casual energy like the energy of a bomb that explodes. It has a guiding principle, a very fine, but unconscious directive, the aim of which is to develop a normal person. When we speak of free children we are thinking of this energy which must be free in order to construct these children well. We must aid this purpose. When we do, we find that the children return to this urgent energy and become normal and when this happens all deviations cease.

This phenomenon comes from the conditions of life and so the cure for difficult children must be to prepare a free life for them, and provide an environment because the environment is part of life and life cannot exist without it. This is an indirect preparation. In the right environment normality comes naturally, by itself. You must realize that you do not get very naughty children transformed suddenly when they are put in the right environment. Each child has his own special form of naughtiness, each child is different and so each child reacts differently. So one day a child will concentrate on a piece of work and after this we will find that he has changed. But your eye must be trained to observe this phenomenon when it happens. We do not generally notice things like this, especially those on the spiritual side. I cannot give you spectacles to see with. When a child concentrates his character is changed. It is as though he had taken off a mask. Suppose you have a class of 30 children who are all disorderly and inattentive except two, who are normal. The teacher must be able to recognize the difference in these children. It is not so easy to see the difference because acts of destruction and disorderliness are so much more noticeable than normal behaviour. The teacher sees the defects. Again, a teacher does not interfere when a child is destroying a piece of material, because she thinks this may be a moment of concentration. People who begin to study biology must study things under a microscope, but until their eyes have been trained they cannot see anything. So the eyes of the teacher must be trained. A sensitivity must be developed in the teacher in order to recognize this ephemeral phenomenon of concentration when it occurs …

1946 (4) The work of the teacher is to guide the children to normalization, to concentration. She is like the sheepdog who goes after the sheep when they stray, who conducts all the sheep inside. The teacher has two tasks: to lead the children to concentration and to help them in their development afterwards. The fundamental help in development, especially with little children of three years of age, is not to interfere. Interference stops activity and stops concentration. But do not apply the rule of non-interference when the children are still the prey of all their different naughtinesses. Don't let them climb on the windows, the furniture etc. You must interfere at this stage. At this stage the teacher must be a policeman. The policeman has to defend the honest citizens from the disturbers. She must not only not interfere when a child is concentrating, she must also see that he is not disturbed. Do what you like with the rest of your class, anything

BASIC IDEAS OF MONTESSORI'S EDUCATIONAL THEORY

you have learnt during your training or anything that your common sense dictates, it is not important because this stage is not important ... and after a time something will come from the hidden soul of the child and he will become concentrated and have a new life. He will become normalized.

Sources: (1) *The Advanced Montessori Method I*, p. 53–57; (2) *The Child in the Family*, p. 30–32; (3) *The Child, Society and the World*, p. 12–13; (4) Ibid., p. 16–17.

III

KEYS TO THE WORLD

A. A New Education: "The Foundations of my Pedagogy"

1934 In every country work is being done to improve education. A range of psychological sciences with the most varied names have emerged which aim to study the child. Most of these studies start from the assumption that the child has a specific nature, recognized as normal, and all their premises and conclusions remain theoretical. Where a discovery was made, there was no way to put this discovery to good use in the life of the child. Yet in most cases it is still believed to this day, despite all the research, that the adult can shape a child's character, and that it is not only the task, but the duty of the teacher to do so. The child and his creative powers are allowed to play only the minutest part in this work of education. Childhood is considered by many educationalists and most parents as a transitional stage on the road to adulthood, and on this basis all the needs of the child's existence are decided by the adult. His character must be strengthened, certain moral qualities must be instilled, other immoral ones suppressed. His mind must be formed and specific cultural values must be taught. The child is required to work in the same way as the adult: purposefully and with the minimum effort. Specific tasks must be completed in specific periods. The child's internal order is dictated from outside, and obedience and discipline are the consequences of adult authority. A child's inner order is only ever of interest if he is ill, highly-strung or more than usually naughty.

Pedagogy, just like medicine, requires education to begin on the first day of life. Medicine demands that the adult consider the child's development, even before he is born, and this is therefore something that only the adult himself can

19

do. Medicine provides guidelines and assistance which we are familiar with in the rules of hygiene and child care, and which are aimed solely at the adult. Pedagogy, however, merely offers a principle, some advice as it were, as to how the adult can perform his own, educational task, as easily as possible. It offers help for the adult, but not for the child. The advice is to start education as early as possible, while the child is still like soft wax, that it is easier to mould the young child from soft wax than it is the older one, who is no longer so yielding. And thus the child is educated from day one, and his mistakes and disobedience are forbidden and punished. It is therefore the adult, and not the child, who enjoys the benefits of pedagogical theory.

If a problem remains difficult to solve in spite of every effort and all the means available, this is often due to the fact that not every individual factor of potential relevance to its solution has been sufficiently taken into account. Once the neglected factor has been discovered, the problem appears surprisingly simple. It is precisely the most obvious factors which are more often than not overlooked.

The personality of the child has only ever been considered from the single pedagogical perspective, in which the child is made the *object* of education and teaching. A certain relationship between the child and the adult has been determined in this pedagogical approach. The nature of these relations has not, however, been sufficiently investigated, yet alone made explicit.

Further investigation reveals a *social problem* which has never been taken into account. The neglected factor has been found. The child and the adult live in a union that produces conflict. They are two completely different beings.

The adult is a determined, dominant individual, in contrast to the little, ignorant child who, in his helplessness, is entrusted to his care. With his labour geared to external production, the adult has created for himself an environment which meets his own needs. The child inhabits this world like an extra-social being who can contribute nothing to this society, since the goal of *his* life and *his* labour lies within him and not in the outside world.

KEYS TO THE WORLD

The child is a stranger in the adult social order who might well declare, "My Kingdom is not of this world".

Pedagogy must therefore make requirements which are aimed at the adult and not at the child.

From this insight into the relation between the child and the adult we have discovered more than an abstract psychology. We have discovered the new child, who has revealed himself to us through wonderful manifestations. We see clearly that childhood is a stage of humanity which differs completely from that of adulthood. We have recognized the two differing forms of man. The child does not bear the scaled-down features of the adult, but develops his own inner life, which has its own purpose. Who is it who brings about this second creation, this making of the adult? Do the parents grow on the child's behalf? Does the educator shape his character? Does the teacher form his mind? The maturation of the man in the child is another type of pregnancy that lasts longer than pregnancy in the womb, and it is the child alone who forms his personality. His creative will urges him to develop. The blueprint of the character is not yet visible in the infant, but the whole of his personality lies within him, as within the cell.

The adult should not strive to achieve the superior manner of a powerful educator, but must organize relations between himself and the child on a harmonious basis, and develop a sympathetic attitude towards the child. Then he will as a matter of course create an environment that is suited to the child's activities, so that the child – the master in this environment – is free to develop. It is necessary for the *adult* to organize and reconcile the two differing rhythms of life, and to understand the limits within which he may act in an educational capacity. It is necessary for him to learn restraint towards the child. We preach moderation and patience as basic preparation for the teacher, and moderation and patience to all mothers and fathers and to all those who come into contact with children. This moderation will not weaken or spoil the child, but will remove the greatest obstacle to the healthy development of his personality.

BASIC IDEAS OF MONTESSORI'S EDUCATIONAL THEORY

We too shall use the comparison with wax, but in a totally different way. It is true that in his early life the child is like soft wax, but this wax can only be shaped by the expanding personality itself. The sole duty of the adult is to preserve this process from any disturbance, so that the fine patterns which the awakening psychical life of the child makes on the wax are not obliterated. The small child shapes language before he is capable of speaking. He shapes movement, before he is familiar with deliberate movement. For the adult to obliterate these delicate patterns is like the waves of the sea pounding against the sand and wiping everything away. And whoever wanted to construct anything here would have to start anew every time, and in so doing would grow weary.

We understand education as assisting the psychical development of the child from birth. We want to protect and care for this child, who must continue to grow, every day and every hour, and whose labour is the greatest creative labour of mankind. Just as his body grows and develops in stages, so his personality also grows in periods of particular sensitivity. The child's entire labour of development is governed by laws we are unfamiliar with, and proceeds at a pace of activity that is alien to us. We make no attempt to fathom these mysterious powers, but we regard them as a secret which belongs to the child alone. The help we are able to offer belongs in the outside world. This requires judicious restraint on the part of the adult, for it is a peculiarity of the relations between the child and the adult – and one that gives the latter unlimited power – that the child always bears a relation to the adult, but never the reverse. We are able to lead our lives even without children, but the child needs the adult in order to live. The *severing* of this relationship is necessary for man's development. A being comes into existence only through separation.

All the child's unconscious efforts are directed to developing as a free personality by separating from the adult and achieving independence. Our education takes account of these efforts in every respect; and it is our endeavour to help the child become independent. How much energy is needed before the small child leaves his mother's side, before he can walk alone and no longer needs to be carried, before he can speak and tell us what he needs and can correctly perform all the actions in his young life on his own, and no longer requires the oppressive help of the adult. We can clearly observe the stages of the child's liberation from the adult: his teeth allow him to feed himself independently of his mother, walking means he is able to move without adult help, and speaking marks the beginning of his ability to communicate, so that he is no longer dependent on the adult to interpret his wishes.

The adult does not take account of this creative effort by the infant. He generally believes that a new-born child is safe if the most rudimentary requirements of hygiene are satisfied. Crying, which as an expression of pain remains with us throughout our lives, is noted with satisfaction as a breathing exercise. How many desires this small creature must have which it is as yet unable to express and which are never understood, and how great its suffering must be when they are not fulfilled!

Those who tend and care for the infant in the first days of its life ought to be given quite different training than they receive today. How gently this little creature should be treated, how peaceful should be its surroundings and how closely it should be watched, in order to satisfy all its needs, which are so immensely important for its whole life. Instead, even in the most loving home and with the best nurse, interest is focused on the things which surround the child and could endanger him, and not on the needs of the little expanding soul. Objects are protected from his small and still awkward hands. Education starts with rebukes and prohibitions, and nobody realizes how many wounds are thus inflicted, instead of creating an environment which takes account of the child's activity. The adult's actions in his relation with the child are not aimed at helping him, but at stifling his activity.

The young child slowly starting to look round at the *outside world* is embarking upon the important period of *observation*. He accumulates one image after another and commits them to memory. The adult can do nothing directly to help in this labour, but he must be constantly aware that he should not disrupt it.

Adults who pick up young children without understanding the expression on their little faces, or who rock or play with a child without knowing what that child actually wants, may well be disturbing him during an important task. A young child needs to observe every new thing attentively for a long time, be it a new human face or an object. How often has a young child cried when interrupted like this, without anyone understanding his tears.

BASIC IDEAS OF MONTESSORI'S EDUCATIONAL THEORY

We allow our young children to make their observations; we do not disturb them while they are gathering these images, which represent their first knowledge of the world.

In order to learn about the outside world and find his way around it, the child needs an *order* which forms part of his life, and which he tries to protect wherever he can. He always loves to see the things in his environment in the same place, and tries hard to reestablish this order if it is ever disturbed.

Yet how rarely we recognize this need on the part of the child. How rarely he is helped here, and how often does such an interruption result in the child's despair and bitter tears! In most cases the adult now believes he has discovered the first fault and hastens to correct it. We, however, recognize in such despair the powerlessness of the young child to make himself understood and give expression to his disappointment. In the family there must be a place which belongs solely to the child and in which things always remain in the same position. What is involved here is not a sense of material possession, as the adult understands it, but a spiritual possession on the part of the child.

A particularly striking feature in the young child is his *memory of movement*. How often, when the adult says something to the child, does the child not understand the words, but remembers the movement, and thus notes what is wanted. How often a child will associate with a word a particular movement performed by the adult when he heard this word for the first time. And how little the adult understands when the young child later makes some movements on hearing this word which are now quite inappropriate. But instead of helping him and using this powerful memory for movement to guide the child, we smile at these incomprehensible curiosities and confuse this attentive little creature, who so earnestly wanted to do the right thing and was so proud of his modest knowledge.

It is so simple to show a young child everyday actions in slow, calm movements, and the outcome will be that at a very early age the child is able to eat, wash and dress on his own and will become a happy and contented person.

KEYS TO THE WORLD

Equally important to the child's development is his *own spontaneous movement*. The child must always be moving around, can only think or pay attention when he is moving. He has shown us this need, but only because we gave him the freedom to express himself.

Observation and hearing are not enough for the child to develop, but he must also be able to move. He will often perform a certain movement many times in succession. This is a necessary exercise to achieve order in the movements and physical posture.

We accordingly endeavour to take account of the child's needs in this relationship. We do not place him in narrow little chairs and barred pens, but give him the opportunity to exercise his little limbs again and again.

Precision and control of movement are developed by the body's motor apparatus, and this is closely connected with the psyche. In order to facilitate this development, which satisfies psychic and physical needs, the child's environment must be simple, compatible with a child's physical dimensions and thereby fully suited to his activity. If an environment is unsuitable for the child, his activity is not wasted, but channelled in the wrong directions. No mother will manage to prevent the movements that her child intends to make. The child does not understand if he is forbidden, for the adult has failed to see the purpose of his movements. Movement was the necessary expression of an inner activity.

The adult is equally unable to understand the fact that when he is entirely free to act a young child often *repeats* his little everyday actions many times. These actions seem to lack purpose, for the adult fails to see the purpose if a child washes his hands twenty times in succession or keeps scrubbing away at a clean table.

This phenomenon of repeated activity occurs in every normal child living under the right conditions. He repeats the exercises again and again, and suddenly stops without any external cause. He probably stops because an inner satisfaction has been attained. Activity on the outside has an inner motive that we cannot see. The young child who begins his action with a purpose very soon forgets this purpose in a new, spontaneous activity generated by the pleasure he derives from the movement. So he scrubs the table ten times, even though it is already clean. The child finishes when the activity is satisfied. Only gradually, when the various movements associated with these actions have been mastered, and the need to perform them diminishes, only then does the purpose, which up to then was only the impetus to action, come to the fore, and elementary activity slowly develops into rational activity and moves ever closer to the purposefulness of the adult.

We see from this that the way the young child works is completely different from that of the adult. The child does not work quickly and purposefully. For the child, things in the outside world are never an accomplished goal, but to him everything is merely a means of forming his personality. All the child's vital energies follow the path that leads to inner fulfilment. So how can we disturb and stop a child who is repeating his little exercises so quietly and contentedly, and try to explain something to him in words he simply does not understand? It is not our job to teach the child to work quickly and purposefully. Any such attempt would be futile. A child who develops undisturbed in the right environment comes to work purposefully entirely of his own accord and in his own good time.

This impulse, which cannot be checked but at the most can be misdirected, is of fundamental importance to our attitude towards the child. We ought not to make light of the child's spontaneous actions because they have no meaning for us, but we must view them as important manifestations of his growth. All the things in the environment which we prepare for the child are so ordered as to present the outward goal to the child in a stimulating manner. The child is invited to commence the action out of interest, and the initial action is then followed by repetition.

The young child has a strong need for *active sensory impressions*. We offer objects to the child which give him the opportunity to satisfy this need much more clearly and easily. We know that the child explores the environment with all his sense organs and selectively absorbs and orders the images. But since we also know that an overcomplicated environment with many incoherent stimuli hinders the child's mental task, we come to his aid by offering him images which are well-ordered and help him to achieve order. We teach the child by giving him a guide which meets his instinctive needs and gives him a feeling of pleasure, because it helps him to perform satisfying work. We offer the child well-ordered stimuli with the *material* and thus do not teach directly, as is usually the case with young children, but rather by means of an order inherent in the material, and which the child can acquire on his own. We must prepare the whole environment, including all material objects, to a degree that the child can perform every activity himself.

We are often attacked by educationalists and psychologists who claim our material is of no use to a child because it is unnatural. They claim the child must be offered everything as naturally as it occurs in the environment, and if a colour is provided, attention should not be focused on the colour itself, because there is always an object of which this colour is characteristic. Colour and object belong together, and the child should regard the colour as one of the many properties of this one object. Our material is not meant to be a substitute for the world and to impart knowledge of the world by itself, but is meant as a help and guide for the child's inner labour. We do not isolate the child from the world, but we give him the mental equipment with which to conquer the whole world and its culture. It is like a key to the world and is not to be confused with the world itself.

Almost always, a young child's activity is *dictated* to him, rather more so in the case of the older child. In all these things we give the child an entirely *free choice*, for we have realized that even in his choice of activity the child is guided by strong inner motives. The child who chooses his activities on his own can express and satisfy an inner need in this way. The child alone knows what is necessary for his development, and an activity which is forced upon him disrupts his development and his equilibrium.

The type of activity our material involves is very different from the usual skills which young children are generally made to perform. Plasticine work, for example, involves making an object. A well-defined goal awakens children's activity, and once the goal is reached, the work is over and the activity must cease. Our material does not offer such a goal. The child works with it and often repeats the exercises numerous times, and only the satisfaction of his inner need puts an end to the activity. If the objects are put back in their place, then no outwardly visible change has occurred, but the usual order is restored. The order of this child's environment provides him with a basis for his inner development. If the child orders his environment, then this outwardly orientated activity indicates the beginnings of inner order. Inner order manifests itself in the need to maintain outer order. This requires precise movements which demand the child's full attention. To allow for this need, all things in the environment, not only the tables and chairs and household utensils but also the dimensions of the rooms, doors and windows, are suited to the child's size. Even without our environment, the child can acquire knowledge of the world, but the environment helps the child to achieve the deep *concentration* that is vital for human development.

Inner concentration is a phenomenon experienced in all our children which is of the greatest importance for inner growth, and which has never previously been included as an essential element in pedagogy. On the contrary, the child's concentration is actually subject to general disruption.

It is as though a child who works with concentration becomes oblivious and distant from the outside world. Nothing can disrupt his work, and if concentration ceases, this results from an inner process. Then the child does not appear tired, but rested and joyful. In young children, concentration only ever appears in association with an external object, and cannot yet be separated from the environment.

We regard this fundamental psychological phenomenon as an important basis for the child's work.

Work is an activity which relates neither to instruction nor to the wishes of the adult. Work *unites the child with the environment*, but this work can be seen only in those children who live in an environment that is *suited* to them. *Enforced* work harms the child because it first gives rise to reluctance to work. In normal schools we find children who become weary from learning and studying and thus try to do as little work as possible. The teacher has to keep them working with a mixture of punishment and praise, and by applying external disciplinary rules. Our children work of their own free will, are full of joy and intensely interested. Work does not tire them, but makes them happy. We leave it to the environment to guide the child in his work, and all the constituents of this environment share a common function: the *control of error*. Since the child has not only an impulse to act, but also to perfect himself, we entrust him, guided as he is by the control of error in his environment, with the consistent perfection of his actions. The child becomes a discoverer of the world and wishes to advance ever further and exploit his discoveries. And what is the history of civilization if not the history of discoveries? It is meaningless to convey the assets of this civilization to the child by words. The essential thing is that he should *experience* them. Everything must be related to the child's inner needs in such a way that it is accessible to the mind of a child, and that the child can advance and develop enthusiasm through his own work. The child's interest is solely dependent on the possibility of making discoveries of his own. For this we provide *intellectual* material which represents man's abstract mental work. The child can work with this as his nature dictates, and it can satisfy his urge to explore and acquire knowledge. This material gives the child the chance to use his intelligence. It is in some ways only a *beginning*, and its use in manual work organizes and clarifies the child's knowledge, leading to independent mental activity. The material facilitates the child's orderly mental development and creates mental discipline. The life of the children in the Children's House and at school guides their inner growth step by step towards its goal.

Thought and action must become one. The expansion of the personality must take place in complete harmony. Man must be able to shape, discipline and form himself at his own pace. Our goal is the health of the psyche, health which in every normal child gives rise to a socially conscious attitude, voluntary discipline, obedience and will-power.

29

BASIC IDEAS OF MONTESSORI'S EDUCATIONAL THEORY

Since in most schools children learn passively, it is deemed necessary to provide rest from mental activity in the form of physical movement, and physical activity takes over from mental activity. Why must one form of tiring action take over from the other?. In nearly all modern schools with passive teaching of children, mind and movement are kept firmly apart, a separation which causes a split in the child's personality. The meaning we attach to movement is a much deeper one, which not only concerns the motor functions of our body, but embraces the whole of man in his corresponding modes of expression.

Two requirements therefore seem to us to be the most important for the education of the child. The *first* concerns the social life of adult and child, and demands the creation of new relationships and a change in the adult's attitude towards the child. It cannot be achieved through study of the sciences of psychology or pedagogy, but only through inner reflexion. The ultimate solution to the question is not to create the necessary environment for children to live; rather we are faced with the *second* moral requirement, which is to recognize that it is the child's creative mission to develop a moral character. This mission must be respected and supported. We know that man has innate tendencies that appear morally inferior. Deep within every human soul is enacted a drama between "the will to be good and the inclination towards evil". If the child's development is inhibited and disrupted by the adult's lack of understanding, then the energies within the child, which are supposed to be divine means for the formation of mankind, are used as a defence against the adult and give rise to the disintegration of the developing personality, to conflict instead of love. All those who are aware of Original Sin in mankind should reinforce the will to be good by loving and respecting the child, instead of supporting the inclination towards evil by educational measures and their consequences. Belief in the child and his creative mission, and recognition of the faults in the adult, and not the science of psychology or the formulation of remote pedagogical objectives, can serve to develop the unity of the child and his moral perfection.

But if the development is disrupted not once, but continuously, as is the fate of nearly every child, this inevitably gives rise to an inner confusion, which, through a hostile stance towards the adult and consequent support for the "inclination towards evil", has many devastating consequences. These children are unable to obey, for obedience implies personal consent, the opportunity of being able to follow. But if the personality developing inside is torn apart, the result is disorder, visible in the discipline of external actions.

Symptoms are particularly noticeable in the child's *movement*: hands which do no work, yet are unable to be still; excited movements which are a danger to everything around him; distraction, shyness, inattentiveness and much else. An infinite number of the characteristics of these developmental disturbances are known to us, and it would be too great a task to list them all and discuss their causes here. Only one thing must be specifically emphasized, namely that these symptoms are mostly regarded as normal, and often even as particularly good qualities in the child. How proud parents and teachers are of a child who possesses a particularly good imagination. They do not realize that this is a symptom of a disorderly mind that seeks without finding, has lost touch with reality and is given to empty fancies, yet builds nothing. Such a child inhabits the images of his own imagination, and the adult thinks, what creative powers are latent in this child! And yet these powers follow a course that leads not to the creative development of man, but to a confusing lack of inner discipline and to division. Only in later years is it noticed that little remains of the so-called creative powers of these children, and that they do not live up to earlier expectations.

The movements of such children are mostly overanimated, confused and aimless. They are incapable of perseverance and attentiveness. They show no interest in anything that is taught. Educators who regard these children as normal encourage their imaginative powers and believe they are developing something good, and yet they are only fostering division. The confused movements worry the adult, and he attempts to suppress and prohibit them in the child. But the child is unable to obey because he has been badly trained.

It does not occur to the adult to organize a disordered organism which has lost its normal functions, but he tries only to suppress the symptoms.

Dependent, bored children, unable to work on their own, represent another type. They want the adult to do everything with them. They are afraid of being alone. Their movements are passive, they seem to need assistance with everything, and they are considered to be especially affectionate and in need of loving care. They have no motor energy, and their minds are prey to inactivity, which is called laziness. All their wishes and actions are decided by the adult.

Many of these children *tell lies*. The lively, imaginative ones do so from the need to tell fanciful stories, the quiet ones out of shyness, to escape decisions, or from faintheartedness. All attempts to correct their faults individually fail, since they arise from a disturbed personality.

How often the desires of these lively, imaginative children, and those of the quiet, dependent ones, remain unfulfilled, because they know no limits, having been unable to experience the real world for themselves. All they do is want, and being unable to satisfy their wants themselves, they try to achieve their wishes by force through the adult. They try in every way, and finally the adult makes concessions, because his resistance weakens, and he says he has spoilt the child. This is the only mistake which the adult ever admits to!

Parents and teachers stand together in combating these faults in the child. They want to rectify them, forbid, criticize and punish them. It is just like blaming a fever patient for having fever. The whole process of education becomes one of continual correction. The adults are convinced that these characteristics are normal in the child, and that they have a duty to teach them moral standards. If they do not achieve an improvement, stern action is taken, and the child's faults are forcibly suppressed through the external constraint of authority. And nobody notices that the child is increasingly being deprived of the chance to fashion himself from within. It is as though the blind spot in th eye of the adult were obscuring the childhood of man.

If we demand *freedom* for the child in our form of education, we are not understood, because people are familiar only with degenerate children, and misunderstand freedom. They think we require that the child be shown indulgence in everything, in his moods, his destructive rage and his apathy. We are often asked, How do you cure moods, lying and shyness? What do you do when children won't eat and won't obey you? Yes, what do we do in response? We are concerned here with faults which even many psychologists regard as normal features of child-life, but which for us are symptoms of psychical affliction, brought about by a lack of any understanding on the part of the adult. It is no longer possible to attend to the symptoms when these deviations are so far advanced. The moods and lies and shyness cannot be treated separately from each other, and treatment must begin at the root of the evil. The child must be given conditions of life which enable him to recover a normal, healthy personality. We must firstly be, as it were, most tender caring doctors, and only when the child is cured can we again be educators. We must enable the child to reorganize his personality. His inner energies must be turned away from distraction by external objects and redirected to the work of inner construction.

What is the first thing we do to help children in their reconstruction? We prepare an *environment* rich in elements of interesting activity. We pioneer a method that offers material superior to that which has hitherto been deemed satisfactory for children of this age.

The child does not know how to create this environment for himself. Only the adult can do it, and this is the only real help which the child can be given.

The *Montessori House* is the calm and sound environment in which the latent energies of the child can make themselves felt. This environment is prepared by the teacher with great care and with a watchful and patient heart. Her attitude is rather like that of the wise virgins, who brought lighted lamps while waiting for the bridegroom. Even the teacher does not know when the child will reveal himself, but she is always prepared. Otherwise she would be like the foolish virgins who let their lamps go out. They did not see the bridegroom come, and he passed by, without stopping.

It is a real, natural life, a life of many children, in whom there develops a socially conscious feeling for one's fellows and an organic sense of community. How often we see teachers from different nursery and other schools look in disbelief at this natural and disciplined organization of a working community of children. Our teacher can leave the class, and there will be no noticeable change, for order here has been created not by the teacher, but by the children. And what our children succeed in doing as a matter of course has never been achieved by the greatest efforts of these adult teachers. These teachers, who have to punish children and force them to work, will always experience a terrible conflict. They want to be kind to the children and are unable to find a way to do so. And slowly they lose sense of what it was they wanted, and start to believe that punishment and compulsion are part of a teacher's job. Such is the fate of all teachers of the old school.

Enthusiasm for work is extremely importance for the healthy development of the child, but can only arise in an environment that is suited to the child's needs, and only in conjunction with an attitude on the part of the teacher which is helpful but not didactic, and which can only be acquired after a long period of study.

The *preparation of the environment* and *the preparation of the teacher* are the practical foundation of our method of education. The teacher's attitude must always remain one of love. Pride of place belongs to the child, and the teacher follows and supports him. He must set aside his own activity in favour of the child. He must become passive, so that the child may become active. He must give the child freedom to express himself, for there is no greater obstacle to the expansion of the child's personality than an adult who sets all his superior strength against him.

With the adult's attitude towards the child, it is a case of *limiting any intervention*. The child must be helped where help is needed, but too much of this help disturbs the child.

Our parents and teachers do not seek out the child's faults in a desire to correct them, but they seek the nature growing below the surface, and help it to develop healthily. We have often been called optimists, and we are accused of having erroneous views about the child and his nature. Yet what we have discovered is so simple and clear. For decades, all the world's children have revealed this side of their nature to us. We have analyzed their faults and in so doing have discovered a fact. The fact that until now the true nature of the child has remained hidden. We are not optimists, but gold prospectors. We know the rocks where gold is present, and we have learnt from children how to extract the fine metal. The attitude of our teachers is not that of fanciful optimists, but is the attitude of love. Someone who does not love sees only the faults in other people, but he who does love fails to see them, and that's why we say that love is blind. But only he who loves is truly sighted. Only he can see and understand the child's tender revelations, and to him a child will be able to show his true nature.

In all modern educationalists, we observe the intention of eliciting something from the child. They wish to create characteristics in children by a form of freedom, or by stimulating spontaneous expression. Do they really believe that an adult can bring these characteristics to the surface? All the means currently in use only serve to set new obstacles in the way of the child and to overwhelm him. No adult can get a child to manifest his deepest nature. A child can only manifest himself when a position of peace, freedom and non-interference has been established which is free from disturbance by the adult.

The opportunity of enhancing the mind and the consummate characteristics of the child only arises when external conditions permit him to work, and when the means to practise are provided. Then the adult must await any manifestations, and must not try to elicit them by direct action. Only when the child has developed something inside him is he able to express himself.

We do not interrupt the activity of the children, and do not expect them suddenly to do arithmetic or anything else instead of reading. People believe that in so doing they are controlling the course of the child's education, but in reality it confuses the child and disrupts his educational development. Neither in the Children's House nor in the school do we have a fixed programme of study. We do not rely on collective teaching. We endeavour to recognize the sensitive periods, those intervals of the child's inner development, and to make full allowance for them. We do not require a child to be constantly receptive, and do not interpret a momentary lapse of attention as a lack of willingness. We know the strength of the child's ability to take things in by accurate observation, an ability which is far more strongly developed in early childhood than it ever is in the adult, and one which lasts for the entire period of language development. We give greatest consideration to this ability, for we have realized that at this age the words of the adult can be a great obstacle to the child's understanding. That is why verbal *instruction* does not figure prominently in our method. In our work, the teacher is not the educator and instructor of the child, but his assistant. He kindly shows the child every exercise, using clear movements and great precision, and thus makes it possible for the child to act by himself. And acting alone becomes an expression of will. Without performing an action, he cannot express his will. The life of the will is that of action. Our children live and act freely and independently in the company of other children, and in this way become strong-willed social creatures who themselves impose ever greater demands on their own actions.

We give the child the cultural assets of his *nation*, which becomes the basis on which he works to acquire his own culture. We give him the opportunity to do a child's type of work. Work is the cornerstone of his freedom. The freedom of our children has as its limit the community, for freedom does not mean doing what one wants, but being master of oneself.

What is the freedom of the child? Freedom is attained when the child can grow by his own inner laws, in accordance with the needs of his development. The child is free when he has gained independence from the oppressive energy of the adult. This liberation is neither an idea nor a utopia, but a fact which is frequently met with, a reality which we continually experience. We do not thereby exclude the need to impart culture, nor the requirement of discipline and the need for teachers. The difference is solely that in this freedom children work happily, and acquire culture through their own activity, that discipline originates from within the child himself.

Children who enter our Children's Houses and schools burdened with the familiar faults are initially disorderly and restless. They disturb themselves and others and run to and fro. But one of the many activities or some item of material very soon arouses their interest, and when they start to repeat one of the exercises, when they show steady concentration and attention during an activity, then we know that reconstruction has begun.

The children's restlessness and confused movements gradually cease. And it is often the case that all the faults disappear at the same time, and not only during the period spent in the Children's House and the school, but also in every area of their lives. The children's laziness disappears. Because of the atmosphere of calm and the feeling that no other will wishes to lead and repress him, because of the freedom he is allowed, a spontaneous activity reawakens in the child and he starts to work happily and with concentration. Shyness and fear disappear. The children become confident and free in their behaviour, and show a natural modesty. Fanciful notions very quickly evaporate, and the mind, which lacked the opportunity to concentrate and was prone to wander, becomes orderly and begins to develop wonderfully. Such a change is not achieved by a forced act of separation from the child's old world, but only by enabling the child to adopt a different attitude to the world about him. We must open up new routes for the whole of the child's inner growth, through which his underlying nature can unfold.

Along with all the familiar faults, we also witness the decline of that excessive dependency on other people which is always detrimental to the child. It is as though natural dignity grew along with self-reliance. The children grow independent and free, and attain a level of control over their personality and particular situations that up to this point was never thought possible in a child.

Adults who have observed these children in our Children's Houses and schools have often said that this transformation borders on the miraculous, and our parents have been heard to speak of Montessori miracles. It is interesting to note the extent to which our children influence their parents. We see time and again how much parents can learn from their children.

In these observations, we have recognized two different types of nature in the child: The familiar one, which is studied by psychologists, which every educationalist has come to expect, and which we call *abnormal*; and the still hidden nature of the child, which we call the *normal* one.

Our work was not based on any branch of psychology, but we have made a great psychological discovery, we have found the normal child.

The child whom we call normal is organically linked to the very beginnings of his own life, and his whole nature, which is in the process of developing, is harmonized through an inner equilibrium. The other type of child is the one whom the adult has not understood, and whose inner growth has been stifled and has taken miserable refuge in division.

How often do we hear the remark that an adult has not lived up to his childhood promise. He has been unable to develop healthily as a child, and his personality has been destroyed.

BASIC IDEAS OF MONTESSORI'S EDUCATIONAL THEORY

The characteristics which I call normal are manifested by children in such a simple, delicate, one might almost say near invisible manner, that they have never been observed before now.

The child has shown us that personal dignity resides in the soul of each of these little human beings, and that a child feels and understands more than the adult suspects. It is just that his means of self-expression are weaker.

Through the adult's new attitude towards the child in the family, the Children's House, and the school, through respect for his creative task, and through the preparation of a revealing environment, the child's energies are concentrated rather than dissipated, and help is given to develop a character whose inner freedom leads to free moral action. A creature of nature becomes a creature of reason, who through concentration and silence grows into a socially conscious individual, and who shapes his moral character in the harmony of thought and movement, of free will and of action. The secret within the child will be the freedom of man.

We require moderation and inner reflection from all teachers. We require respect for the child from the first day of his life, so that degenerate children do not become degenerate adults, but so that the normal child we have identified may bring his blessing upon mankind.

Education should not just help the child to fulfil the great task of becoming a human being, but it bears responsibility for the physical and psychical health of mankind.

The faults of child growth and their consequences are so universally known and so general that it might almost be said that the organization of human development has not yet been witnessed in the world. Man does many great things, but there is one thing he achieves only rarely: the inner discipline of character. We have seen that this mystery is resolved much more easily by a child than by the adult, and thus the healthy child can offer us the marvellous image of an innerly ordered human being.

The health or sickness of the soul, the strength or weakness of the character, and the clarity or confusion of the mind depend solely on the harmonious and peaceful development of the child's psyche. A child whose development has been in the form of slavery will not become an adult who achieves great things.

Source: Grundlagen meiner Pädagogik (here reproduced in unabridged form).

B. Key Concepts of Montessori's Pedagogy

1. "Milk and Love": The "Psychic Embryo"

1949 (1) Could we not call the child, who in appearance only is psychically inert, an *embryo*, in whom the psychical powers and organs of man are being developed? He is an embryo in whom exists nothing but nebulae which have the power to develop spontaneously certainly, but only *at the expense of the environment* – an environment rich in greatly different forms of civilization. That is why the human embryo must be *born* before completing itself and why it can reach further development only after birth. Its potentialities, in fact, must be stimulated by the environment.

There will be many "inner influences" just as in physical growth there are many, especially during the processes depending on the genes, e.g. the influence of various hormones. In the spiritual embryo, instead, there are directing *sensitivities*. In the case of language the examination of the sense-organs reveals that the sense of hearing seems to be the least developed during the first weeks of life. Yet the most delicate sounds which compose a word have to be received through that very sense. It appears, therefore, that the ear does not merely *hear* as a sense-organ, but is guided by special sensitivities to collect the sounds of human speech only from the environment. These sounds are not merely heard, they provoke motor reactions in the delicate fibres of the vocal cords – the tongues, lips etc. Thus among all the muscle-fibres it is those of the speech-organs which are aroused to reproduce these sounds. Nevertheless, this is not

39

immediately revealed, but stored away until that time when language is to be born, just as the child during intra-uterine life is being formed without functioning and is then, at a given moment, stimulated to enter the world and starts functioning all of a sudden.

These, of course, are suppositions, but the fact remains that there are inner developments, *directed* by creative energies, and that these developments can reach maturity before they become outwardly manifest.

When they finally reveal themselves they are *characteristics* already built up to form part of the individuality of the person ...

1910 (2) ... Pleasurable psychical stimulation assists physical development through the expansion of healthy activities.

When we are concerned with influencing the physiological growth of children, these viewpoints should be carefully noted. Fénelon recounts a fable about a she-bear and her exceptionally ugly cub. On the advice of a crow, she licked and caressed it so fervently that it finally developed into a magnificent and handsome bear. Underlying this fable is the idea that by her love, a mother can change the body of her child, and help him develop harmony through the psychical stimuli of affection and encouragement.

Nature has not only provided the mother with milk, the child's physical sustenance, but has in addition made her capable of that absolutely altruistic form of love which transforms her soul, and liberates moral powers which the mother herself never knew of or suspected – just as the sweet, nutritious particles of milk were formerly unknown to the red blood corpuscles. Thus does human nature provide for the preservation of the species in two ways, and only the combination of the two results in full human nourishment: food and love. When a child is weaned, he receives nourishment from his environment in a specific form, but a wealth of psychical stimuli likewise derive from this environment which not only shape his psychical personality, but just as surely bring about the full development of his physiological personality.

KEYS TO THE WORLD

I was able to gain meaningful experience of this in the "Children's Houses" in the San Lorenzo district of Rome. This is the poorest part of the city, and the children there are the sons and daughters of day-labourers, who consequently are often unemployed. Even today, illiteracy amongst adults is still so incredibly common that in a very high percentage of all cases at least one parent is unable to read. In these "Children's Houses" we take in young children between the ages of 3 and 7 for a period which varies between nine to five o'clock in the summer and and nine to four in the winter.

We have never provided meals in the school. The little children, who all live at home with their parents, have half an hour's break in which they can go home to eat. Thus we have not influenced their diet in any way.

Our pedagogical methods however are chosen to represent an incremental series of psychical stimuli perfectly suited to the needs of a child. The environment stimulates each pupil to the level of psychical development that is individually suited to him and in keeping with what he subjectively feels to be possible. The children have complete freedom of expression and are treated with great affection. I believe that this is the first time that this extraordinarily interesting pedagogical experiment has been performed: to sow the seed in the child's consciousness, to allow the spontaneous expansion of his personality in the most extreme sense, in an environment which is calm and warmed by a feeling of affection and peace.

The results were astonishing. We had to revise our views on child psychology, because many of the so-called instincts of childhood did not develop at all, but instead unforeseen emotions and mental impulses appeared at the very earliest stages of the consciousness of these children: true revelations of the sublime grandeur of the human soul! The mental alertness of these children was like a spring of water shooting up from beneath the rocks which had inadvertently been lying on top of their burgeoning souls. We saw how they managed the incredible, and spurned their toys in a totally insatiable thirst for knowledge. We saw how these children, who were said to have the instincts of vandals, took care of the most fragile teaching material,the most delicate plants. In short, they appeared to embody the childhood of a human race that was more highly developed than the one to which we belonged. And yet they belong to that same humanity, miraculously guided and stimulated by their own natural and free development.

Even more astounding however is the fact that the children's general state of nutrition improved so much that today their outward appearance differs considerably from before, and from the present state of their brothers (children of the same age). Many of the weakly children have been physically strengthened, and a large number of lymphatic types have been cured. In general, all the children have put on weight and appear in such perfect health that they look like the children of rich parents from the country. Nobody who saw them would suspect that these are the children of illiterates from the lowest class. Let us now take a look at some notes which we made about these children when they first entered our school. The vast majority were noted as being of weak constitution, but none of them received medication or a change of diet. The strength which the children regained was solely the consequence of a fully satisfied psychical existence. And yet for eleven months of the year they remain at school the whole time from 9 to 5 every day. It might be said that this is an extraordinarily long teaching time, but what is more amazing is the fact that the children remain "active" throughout this entire time; and more remarkable still, as many of their mothers can report, is that their little ones continue to work tirelessly at home until bed time. Finally, however – and this seems almost unbelievable – many of the children are already back at school by about 8.30 in the morning. They smile peacefully, as if happily anticipating the pleasure awaiting them during the long day to come! We have seen little boys reacting consciously to the things around them, filled with spontaneous joy at their new experiences. Their size, which we measure on a monthly basis, shows us the powerful stirrings of physiological growth in each of them, and the exceptional regeneration of the blood in some.

KEYS TO THE WORLD

The fact that our experiment produced such a result astonished us as an unexpected revelation of nature, or, to put it another way, as a scientific discovery. Nevertheless, we could have foreseen something of all this if we had considered for a moment how our own physical health depends far more on our contentment and happiness, and on a clear conscience, than on that material substance we call bread.

Let us learn to recognize the man, sublime in his true reality, let us learn to recognize him in the most delicate child. We have shown by our experiments that he develops through work, freedom, and love. Hitherto we have stifled the marvellous potentialities of his nature with silly toys and slavish discipline, and we have ignored his manifestations of spontaneity. From his earliest childhood he lives in order to learn, to love and to be productive. From this his bones derive their growth, and his blood its vitality.

All such potentialities for physiological development are being stifled by our antiquated pedagogical methods. More or less completely, they impede the development of independent personalities, to confine all pupils within identical limits. The development of the individual is hindered by the fact that everyone is expected to adopt these limits. The pupil is forced to accept from us, instead of using his own potential to be productive. He is forced to sit still, and just as his body is bound to the iron frame of the desk, so his mind is bound to a strict programme of teaching.

We would like to see them as machines that are powered and controlled by us, where in reality they are the most sensitive and perfect creation of nature.

We are destroying divine powers through slavery. We use reward and punishment as a scourge to demand submission from these gloriously independent spirits. We encourage them with rewards, but to what purpose? So that they can win prizes. All right, but in so doing we encourage the child to lose sight of his true goal of knowledge, freedom and work. We dazzle him with a prize which from the moral perspective signifies vanity, but materially amounts to no more than a few grammes of metal. We prescribe punishments in order to

43

put down rebellious nature, who however is rebelling not against goodness and beauty, against the meaning and purpose of life, but against us, we who are tyrants instead of advisers.

And let us not likewise punish disease, misfortune and poverty!

We are not educators of men, but are forcing our way into the domain of human freedom.

Our belief in reward and punishment as necessary means for the advancement of children and the maintenance of discipline is a delusion, and has been shown as such in experiments. Vain material reward for a few children is not the psychical stimulus which spurs on the diverse development of human life to greater heights. Rewards reduce splendid self-confidence in man to mere vanity and impose upon it the bonds of egotism, i.e. of damnation. The only stimulus worthy of man is the pleasure he derives from being conscious of his own growth. And he grows only by conquering his own mind and by spreading universal friendship. It is wrong that a child should not be able to feel an intellectual stimulus far greater than that wretched prize which gives him an egotistical and deceptive sense of superiority over his fellow-pupils. It is probably the case that, corrupted as we are by our own egotism, we measure these new powers of surging human life by our own narrow standards.

The little boys and girls in our "Children's House" are instinctively suspicious of rewards. They ignore the little medals which are pinned to the chest as prizes, and instead look out for things to work with, by which, without any guidance from the teacher, they can form, judge and correct themselves, and thus work towards perfection.

As for punishment, it has an oppressive effect, and is imposed on children who are already oppressed.

Even in the case of strong, grown-up men, we know it is necessary to encourage the fallen, help the weak, and console the disheartened. If such methods are right for adults, then how much more they are needed by those who are still developing!

This is the great reform which the world expects from us: to break the iron chains with which we have been holding down the spirit of generations of young people ...

1938 (3) The incarnate child is a spiritual embryo that must live at the expense of its environment. Just as the physical embryo requires the special surroundings of the womb, so the spiritual embryo also needs the protection of a living environment warmed by love and rich in sustenance, in which everything is designed to foster its growth and there are no obstacles in its way.

Once the adult has understood this fact, his behaviour towards the child must undergo a fundamental change. The child as a spiritual embryo that is about to become incarnate cannot fail to unsettle us, and imposes new responsibility upon us.

This little, delicate, charming creature which we admire and entrust to purely physical care, which our hands treat almost like a toy, all at once becomes something that calls for our deep respect. *"Multa debetur puero reverentia"*.

This incarnation takes place amid secret toil. All around this labour of creation, an unknown drama is being enacted.

No other creature is in the position of having to want before it has a proper will, of having to give orders, so that activity and discipline appear in inert matter. A precarious, delicate life has just advanced to the threshold of consciousness, and already the senses are establishing contact with their environment and the will is commanding the muscles.

There is an interplay between the individual, or rather the spiritual embryo, and its environment, and in this interplay the individual forms and completes himself. This initial formative activity corresponds to the function of the vesicle that at first represents the heart in the physical embryo and ensures the development and nourishment of all parts of the embryonic body, while taking the required nutrients from the mother's blood vessels. Psychic individuality also develops through the action of this motive principle, which maintains the relation with the environment. All the child's efforts are aimed at absorbing his environment and from these endeavours springs the deep-seated unity of his personality.

During this slow and gradual process, the spirit watches constantly over its instrument, in order to preserve its sovereignty and prevent movement giving way to inertia or becoming mechanical. It must continually command, so that movement may free itself from the control of fixed instincts and yet not end in chaos. These efforts bring about the development of continually fresh constructive energies in the child, and thus contribute to the unceasing labour of spiritual incarnation.

Thus the human personality creates itself, and the embryo, the child, becomes the creator of the man, the *father of the man.*

What have the father and mother really done?

The father's contribution is confined to a single, invisible cell. In addition to a germ cell, the mother has provided the appropriate living environment with everything required for protection and development, so that the germ cell can quietly divide on its own and finally produce the newborn child. It is therefore not quite correct to speak of the father and mother as the creators of the child. Rather we should say: The architect of the man is the child. The child is the father of the man.

The effort which the child secretly expends in pursuit of this goal should be respected as sacred, and we should take an optimistic and expectant attitude towards it. After all, during this period the future personality of the individual is being formed.

The adult's responsibility is so great that it is his duty to investigate the child's psychic needs with due scientific care and to prepare an appropriate environment for him.

(4) ... The secret wholly lies in two words: milk and love ...
1949

1949 (5) It follows that the newborn child has to do a piece of formative work which corresponds in the psychological sphere to the one just done by the embryo in the physical sphere. Before him there is a period of life different from that which he led in the womb; yet still unlike that of the man he is to become. This postnatal work is a constructive activity which is carried on in what may be called the "formative period", and it makes the baby into a kind of "Spiritual Embryo".

Man seems to have two embryonic periods. One is prenatal, like that of the animals; the other is postnatal and only man has this. The prolonged infancy of man separates him entirely from the animals, and this is the meaning we must give to it. It forms a complete barrier, whereby man is seen as being different from all others. His powers are are neither continuations, nor derivations from those of the animals. His appearance on earth was a jump in life: the starting point for new destinies.

What causes us to distinguish between species is always their differences, never their likeness. What constitutes another species is always *something new*. It is not merely derived from the old, but it shows originality. It bears characteristics that never existed before. A new impulse has appeared in the kingdom of the living.

So it was when mammals and birds came into existence. They bore with them *novelties*. They were not mere copies, or adaptations, or continuations of earlier creatures. New features that appeared when dinosaurs became extinct, were, in the birds, the passionate defence of their eggs, the building of nests, the care of the fledglings and their courageous protection. The insensitive reptiles, on the contrary, had always abandoned their eggs. And the mammals surpassed even the birds in their defence of the species. They built no nests, but they let their young grow in their own bodies, and fed them with their blood.

These were quite new biological features.

Then came another new character, that of being human. The human species has a double embryonic life. It is built to a new design, and has a fresh destiny in relation to other creatures.

This is the point at which we must pause, and make a fresh start in all our studies of child development, and of man on his psychological side. If the work of man on the earth is related to his spirit, to his creative intelligence, then his spirit and his intelligence must be the fulcrum of his existence, and of all the workings of his body. About this fulcrum his behaviour is organized, even his physical economy. The whole man develops within a kind of spiritual halo.[1]

Today, even our Western ideas have become receptive to this idea, which has ever been prominent in Indian philosophy. Experience itself has forced us to notice that physical disturbances are often caused by psychological states, the spirit no longer exercising proper control.

If the nature of man is to be ruled by a "spiritual halo[2] which enfolds him", if he depends on this and all his behaviour derives from it, then the first care given to the newborn babe – overriding all others – must be a care for his mental life, and not just for his bodily life, which is the rule today.

The developing child not only acquires the faculties of man: strength, intelligence, language; but, at the same time, he adapts the being he is constructing to the conditions of the world about him. And this it is that gives virtue to his particular form of psychology, which is so different from that of adults. The child has a different relation to his environment from ours. Adults admire their environment; they can remember it and think about it; but the child absorbs it. The things he sees are not just remembered; they form part of his soul. He incarnates in himself all in the world about him that his eyes see and his ears hear. In us the same things produce no change, but the child is transformed by them. We adults merely record the environment in our memory, while the child adapts to his environment. This vital kind of memory, which does not consciously remember, but absorbs images into the individual's very

---

[1] Montessori here employs the word "halo", which is also used in psychology, in a quite special sense (Ed.).

[2] See note 1 (Ed.).

life, has been given a special name by Sir Percy Nunn, who calls it the "Mneme".[3]

One example of this, as we have seen, is language. The child does not "remember" sounds, but he incarnates them, and can then produce them to perfection. He speaks his language according to its complex rules, with all their exceptions, not because he has studied it, nor by the ordinary use of memory. Perhaps his memory never retains it consciously, and yet this language comes to form part of his psychic life and of himself. Undoubtedly, we are dealing with a phenomenon different from the purely mnemonic activity; we are dealing with one of the strangest aspects of the infant mind. There is in the child a special kind of sensitivity which leads him to absorb everything about him, and it is this work of observing and absorbing that alone enables him to adapt himself to life. He does it in virtue of an unconscious power that only exists in childhood.

The first period of the child's life is one of adaptation. We must understand clearly what is meant by adaptation in this sense and distinguish it from the kind of adaptation made by adults. It is the child's biological adaptability that makes the land into which he is born the only one in which he will ever want to live, just as the only language he can speak to perfection will be his mother tongue. A grown-up who lives abroad, never adapts his life in the same way and to the same degree. Think of the missionaries. These are people who go, of their own free will, to carry on their vocation in distant lands, and, if you ask them, they say, "We sacrifice our lives by living here". It is a confession which shows the limitation in the adult's capacity to adapt.

But, turn to the child. He comes to love the land into which he is born, no matter where it is. However hard the life may

---

[3] The word, *Mneme*, in this order of ideas, was first introduced by the German biologist, Richard Semon, but Sir Percy Nunn developed and extended the idea in his *Hormic Theory*. It is in his sense that we use the word, as with his other concepts: *Horme and Engrams*. For futher reference the reader is advised to consult Sir Percy Nunn's excellent book, *Education, its Data and First Principles*, London (1st ed. 1920).

be there, he can never find equal happiness elsewhere. One man loves the frozen plains of Finland, another the sand-dunes of Holland. Each has received this adaptation, this love of country, from the child he used to be.

It is the child who brings it about, and the adult finds himself possessed of it. He then feels he belongs to this country; he is obliged to love it, to feel its fascination; nowhere else does he find the same peace and happiness.

At one time in Italy, those born in the villages lived and died there, without ever going far away. After Italy had become a nation, many, for reasons of marriage or work, left their birthplaces; but in later life, these often suffered from a peculiar illness: pallor, depression, weakness, anaemia. Many cures were tried, and, as a last resort, the doctor would advise the sufferer to go back and take the air of his native parts. And nearly always this advice had the best results; the patients regained their colour and health. People used to say that a man's own air was the best cure, even if the climate he went to was far worse than the one he left. But what these sufferers really needed was the peace offered to their subconscious minds by the simple places where they had lived as children.

Nothing has more importance for us than this absorbent form of mind, which shapes the adult and adapts him to any kind of social order, climate or country. On this, the whole of our study is based. It is opportune to reflect that anyone who says, "I love my country", does not say something superficial or artificial, but reveals a basic part of himself and of his life.

We can therefore understand how the child, thanks to his peculiar psyche, absorbs the customs and habits of the land in which he lives, until he has formed the typical individual of his place and time. The local manner is another of the mysterious formations that a man builds up in childhood. That the customs, and special mentality, of a district are acquisitions is clear enough, since none of these can be natural, or inborn.[4] So we are beginning to gain a much more

---

[4] A convincing proof of this truth can be found in the book by Ruth Benedict, *Patterns of Culture*, New York, 1948.

comprehensive picture of the child's activity. He develops a behaviour not only adapted to this time and region, but also to the local mentality. Thus, the respect for life in India is so great that animals also are included in a veneration firmly rooted in the hearts of the people. So deep a sentiment can never be acquired by people already grown-up. Just to say: "Life is worthy of respect", does not make this feeling ours. I might think the Indians were right; that I also should respect animals. But in me this would only be a piece of reasoning; it would not stir my emotions. That kind of veneration which Indians have for the cow, for example, we Europeans can never experience. Nor can the native Indian, reason as he may, ever rid himself of it. These mental characteristics seem to be hereditary, but really they are infantile formations derived from the child's surroundings. Once in a garden attached to the local Montessori school, we saw a small Hindu child of little more than two, who was looking intently at the ground on which he seemed to be tracing a line with his finger. There was an ant there which had lost two legs and could only walk with difficulty. The child had noticed its predicament, and was trying to be helpful, by making a track for it with his finger. Anyone would have supposed that this Hindu baby must have "inherited" such a fondness for animals

Another child, attracted by these same doings, now approached, saw the ant, put his foot out and crushed it. This second child was a Moslem. A Christian child would possibly have done the same thing, or would have passed on indifferently. One would be forgiven for thinking that here, too – in this feeling of a barrier separating us from the animals, whereby love and respect are due only to men – we had an example of heredity in the mind.

The nations of the world have different religions, but even when the mind of a people comes to repudiate one of its ancient tenets, the heart feels strangely perturbed. These beliefs and feelings form an integral part of ourselves. As we say in Europe: "They are in our blood". All the social and moral habits that shape a man's personality, the sentiments of caste, and all kinds of other feelings, that make him a typical Indian, a typical Italian, or a typical Englishman, are formed during infancy, in virtue of that mysterious mental power that psychologists have called "Mneme".

This holds good, also, for the habitual tricks of posture, bearing and gait which distinguish so many racial types. There are African natives who acquire a special physique for coping with wild beasts. Others perform instinctively the right exercises for sharpening their hearing, so that auditory acuteness marks all those of their tribe. Every personal trait absorbed by the child becomes fixed forever, and even if reason later disclaims it, something of it remains in the subconscious mind. For nothing that is formed in infancy can ever be wholly eradicated. The "Mneme" (that we may think of as a superior kind of memory), not only creates the individual's special characteristics, but keeps them alive in him. What the child had absorbed, remains, a final ingredient of his personality. And the same thing happens with his limbs and organs, so that every grown-up person has an individuality indelibly stamped upon him in this early period of life.

The hope of altering adults is therefore vain. When we say, "This person is not well-bred", or when we remark on another's slovenly deportment, we can easily hurt or humiliate them; make them conscious of their defects. But the faults remain, for they are ingrained and unchangeable.

The same thing explains man's adaptation – let us call it – to the various historical epochs; for, while an adult of ancient times could not live in the world of our day, the child adapts to civilization at the level it has reached when he enters it. Whatever that level may be, he succeeds in making a man who can live there in conformity with its customs. This shows that the true function of infancy, in the ontogenesis of man, is an adaptive one; to construct a model of behaviour, which renders him free to act in the world about him and to influence it.

Today, therefore, the child must be considered as a point of union, a link joining the different epochs of history, the different levels of civilization. Infancy is a period of true importance, because, when we want to infuse new ideas, to modify or better the habits and customs of a people, to breathe new vigour into its national traits, we must use the child as our vehicle; for little can be accomplished with adults. If we really aspire to better things, at spreading the light of civilization more widely in a given populace, it is to the children we must turn to achieve these ends.

Toward the end of the British occupation of India, a family of British diplomats often sent their two children, with an Indian nurse, to have a meal in one of the Indian *hotels de luxe*. There, the nurse, seated on the ground, taught the children to eat rice with their hands, in the Indian manner. The idea was that the children should grow up free from the contempt and repugnance that this national habit of the Indians generally excites in Europeans. For it is these differences of daily life, and the hostile feelings they arouse, that are the main causes of friction between men. If, again, modern customs are felt to be degenerate, and the revival of older ones is desired, nothing effective can be done except through the children. Nothing can be expected from adults. To influence society we must turn our attention to childhood. Out of this truth comes the importance of nursery schools, for it is the little ones who are building mankind, and they can work only on the materials we give them.

The immense influence that education can exert through children, has the environment for its instrument, for the child absorbs his environment, takes everything from it, and incarnates it in himself. With his unlimited possibilities, he can well be the transformer of humanity, just as he is its creator. The child brings us a great hope and a new vision. There is much that we teachers can do to bring humanity to a deeper understanding, to a higher well-being, and to a greater spitituality.

This means the child, from birth, must be regarded as a being possessed of an important mental life, and we must treat him accordingly. Today the mental life of newly born children is, in fact, receiving much more attention. So interesting has it become to psychologists that it seems likely to give rise to a new science – a thing we have already seen happen for the child's bodily life, in the form of hygiene and and pediatrics.

But if a mental life exists even in the newborn babe, this must be already there, otherwise it could not exist. In fact, it must also be present in the embryo, and, when this idea first gained acceptance, the question naturally arose as to when, in the embryonic life, mental life could be said to start. As we know, a child is sometimes born at seven months instead of at nine – and at seven months he is already complete enough to be able to live. So his psyche – like that of the nine months old child – must be able to function. This example, on which I need not dwell, serves to show my meaning when I maintain that all life is psychic. Every species of living creature is endowed in some measure with psychic energy, with a certain kind of psychology, however primitive the creature may be. If we observe unicellular creatures, we see that even they give impressions of awareness; they move away from danger, toward food, and so on.

Yet the baby, till quite a short time ago, was credited with having no mental life; and only recently have mental traits of his, previously not noticed, been admitted to the scientific picture.

Certain facts have come to shine out, and these form new points of light in the adult conscience. They indicate responsibilities that lie within us. The event of birth itself has suddenly struck people's imaginations; and we see the results not only in psychology but also in literature.

Psychologists now speak of the "difficult adventure of birth", referring not to the mother but to the child; the child who suffers without being able to protest, who cries out only when his agony and travail are over.

To be forced to adapt suddenly to an environment totally different from the one in which he has been living, to be obliged to assume on the spot functions never before exercised, and to do this in the unspeakably exhausted state in which he finds himself – this is the hardest and most dramatic test in the whole of a man's life. So say modern psychologists, who have coined the phrase, "birth-terror"[5] to indicate this critical and decisive moment in the child's mental life.

We are not, of course, dealing with a conscious fear, but if the child's mind could speak, it would find words like this to convey the situation: "Why have you thrown me into this dreadful world? What shall I do? How can I live in this new way? How am I to bear all these frightful noises, I, who have never heard so much as a whisper? How can I to take over these difficult functions, which you, my mother, have been doing for me? How do I digest and breathe? How can I bear these frantic changes in climate, I, who have always enjoyed the moderate and unchanging temperature of your body?"

The child is unaware of what has happened. He could not know he was suffering the pangs of birth. Yet there must remain in his soul some mark even if unconscious; he feels in his subconscious mind something of what I have tried to express.

So, those working in this field find it natural to believe that ways must exist of helping the child to make his first adaptation to the world. Let us never forget that the tiniest babies are able to experience fear. When, in the first hours of life, they are dipped rapidly into a bath, they are seen, very often, to make grasping movements, as if they felt themselves to be falling. This is a typical reaction of fear. How does nature help the newly-born? She certainly makes some provision: for example, she gives the mother an instinct to press the little one tightly to her bosom. This protects it from the light. And the mother herself is kept barren for a time. Keeping still for her own benefit, she communicates the necessary calm to her child. Everything happens as if the mother unconsciously realized the damage done to her baby. Holding

---

[5] This phrase was first used in 1923 by Otto Rank, one of the early disciples of Freud, in his theory of "the trauma of birth". Although the whole theory has not been generally accepted, the concept of birth-fear, or terror, has an established place today in the field of depth psychology.

him tightly, she gives him of her warmth, and protects him from too many sensations.

In human mothers, these protective measures are not so vigorously pursued as in animal mothers. We see, for example, how the mother cat hides her kittens in dark corners, and is restive when anyone comes near. The human mother's protective instinct is not so strong, and is therefore more easily lost. Hardly is the child born than someone else takes it away, washes it, dresses it, holds it to the light, the better to see the colour of its eyes, always treating it more like an inanimate object than a living being. It is no longer nature that directs, but human reason, and this acts fallaciously because not illuminated by understanding, and because of the habit we have of thinking the child has no mental life.

It is clear that this period, or, rather, this brief moment of birth, must be considered separately.

It does not concern the child's psychic life in general. It is an episode – his first encounter with the outer world. Natural history shows how cleverly nature provides for this period in mammals. Just before giving her young to the light, the mother isolates herself from the rest of the herd, and she remains apart with her young for some time after their birth. This is most noticeable in animals which live in large herds or packs, such as horses, cows, elephants, wolves, deer and dogs. All these do the same thing. During the period of isolation, the little youngsters have time to adapt themselves to their surroundings. They live alone with their mother, who envelops them in her love, watching over and protecting them. In this phase the little animal comes by degrees to behave like others of its species. During this short period of isolation, there is a continuous psychological reaction, on the part of the little one, to environmental stimuli, and these reactions follow the general plan of behaviour proper to the species. Thus, when the mother rejoins the others, the little one can enter the community already prepared to live as part of it, and this, not just physically speaking, but also in the psychological sense; the young creature's behaviour is that of a little horse, a little wolf, a little calf etc.

KEYS TO THE WORLD

We may note that, even when domesticated, the mammals keep their old instincts in this respect. In our homes we see dogs and cats hide their young with their bodies. By this they are continuing the instincts of the wild, and an intimacy is preserved which keeps the newborn attached to its mother. The nursling, we may say, has left its mother's body but is still one with it. No more practical help could have been devised for making the first way of life give place gradually to the second.

Today, therefore, we have to interpret this vital phase as follows: the animal's racial instincts awaken in the first days of its life.

It is not that difficult circumstances merely arouse or stimulate instinctive responses suited to the occasion and limited by it, but the acts we see form a part of the very plan of creation itself.

If this happens with animals, something like it must also happen with man. What we are dealing with is not just a difficult moment, but a *decisive* moment for the whole of the future. What is now taking place is a kind of awakening of potential powers. These will have the task of directing the huge creative work to be done by the child, by this "spiritual embryo". And, because nature puts evident physical signs at each momentous change in the development of the psyche, so we see the umbilical cord, which kept the child attached to its mother, come away a few days after birth. This first phase is of the utmost importance, for during that phase mysterious powers are in preparation.

So what we have to bear in mind, is not only the *trauma* of birth – but the possibility, or otherwise, of setting in train those activities which must nesessarily follow it. For, although no definite forms of behaviour are pre-established in the child (as they are in the animals), he must neverthe-less possess the power to create a behaviour. There will be no atavistic memories to guide him, but the child will neverthe-less experience *nebulous urges without form*, yet charged with potential energy; and these will have the duty of direct-ing, and incarnating in him, the form of human conduct

57

which he finds in his surroundings. We have called these formless urges, "nebulae".[6] The task of adaptation, the vital task of early childhood, may be compared with the hereditary behaviour "patterns" in the animal embryo. When an animal is born, it is equipped by heredity; it will come by nature to have the right kinds of movement, the needed control, the power to select appropriate food, the forms of defence proper to its kind.

But man has to prepare all this during the general unfolding of his social life; and so the the child, after he is born, has to incorporate into his life all these practices of his social group. Instead of being born possessed of them, he has to absorb them from outside himself.

Sources: (1) *The Formation of Man*, p. 60–61; (2) *Pedagogical Anthropology*, p. 142–145; (3) *Kinder sind anders*, p. 56–58; (4) *The Formation of Man*, p. 69; (5) *The Absorbent Mind*, p. 55–65.

2. The Child and the World: The "Absorbent Mind" and the "Sensitive Periods"

1949 (1) Certainly these complicated processes do not at all follow the procedure established in the adult mind. The child has not learned a language as we would learn a foreign tongue by an effort of our conscious mental faculties. He has yet achieved an exact, firm and marvellous construction like the embryonic constructions of an organ that forms part of a whole organism.

There exists in the small child an unconscious mental state which is of a creative nature. We have called it the "Absorbent Mind". This absorbent mind does not construct with a voluntary effort, but according to the lead of "inner sensitivities" which we call "sensitive periods" as the sensitivity

---

[6] The awakening of the "nebulae" corresponds to the awakening of what are called "behaviour instincts" in the animals, and it happens in the first days of life, those which mental hygiene is obliged to regard as the most important. See *The Formation of Man: Nebulae and World Illiteracy*, by Dr. Maria Montessori, T.P.H., Adyar, Madras, 1955.

lasts only for a definite period, i.e until the acquisition to be made according to natural development has been achieved. Thus if the nebula for language met with obstacles in its development and the constructive acoustic sensitivity did not function, a deaf-mute would be the result, though his organs of hearing and speech would be perfectly normal.

It is clear that there must be a secret fact in the psychic "creation" of man. If we learn everything through attention, volition and intelligence, how then can the child undertake his great construction as he is not yet endowed with intelligence, will-power or attention? It is evident that in him there acts a mind totally different from ours and that, therefore, a psychic functioning different from that of the conscious mind can exist in the unconscious.

The acquisition of a language can serve as the most suitable example to give us an idea of this difference in mentality because language lends itself to study by direct and detailed observation.

The unconscious mind does not register any of the difficulties we experience with regard to different languages which make us refer to some of them as easy and to others as extremely complicated. Evidently this absence of difficulties eliminates, therefore, gradual steps in the mastery of such difficulties. The *whole* language is taken in and always in the same period of time, independently of its simplicity or complication, as judged by the adult mind. This total acquisition of a language cannot be compared to the effort made by the *memory* when we learn a language, neither need we consider the lack of retentivity of the memory which is evident in the case of the adult who easily lets his ephemeral acquisitions slip from him. In the period of unconscious activity language is indelibly stamped upon the mind and becomes a *characteristic* which man finds established in himself. No language that one may wish to add to the mother-tongue can become a characteristic and none will be so sure a possession as the first.

The case is very different with the adult who has to learn a language with his conscious mind. Evidently it is quite easy to learn a primitive language with a simple grammar, like some languages of the peoples of Central Africa, which are often learned by missionaries during their journey across the ocean and deserts on their way to their destination. It is, on the contrary, very difficult to learn a complicated language like Latin, German or Sanskrit. Students take four, five or even eight years to study them, without knowing them perfectly even then. A living, but foreign language, is never entirely mastered – some grammatical mistake or "foreign accent" reveals that one is not speaking one's mother tongue. Further, if this foreign language is not kept in continuous practice it is easily forgotten.

One's mother tongue is not entrusted to the conscious memory. It is deposited in a different memory similar to that which modern psychologists, biologists, and psychoanalysts call the "mneme" or "vital memory". It is supposed by some to contain what is transmitted by heredity through an infinity of time and is considered a "vital power".

A superficial comparison will, perhaps, illustrate this difference. Let us a compare a photograph and a graphic reproduction made the hand and intelligence together, in other words, by writing, drawing or painting. A camera, with its sensitive film, can in a single instant take in anything that comes to it through light. There is no greater effort involved in taking a photograph of a whole forest than in taking that of an isolated tree. A group of people with their background are as easily photographed as a single face. Whatever the complication of the figure, the camera always takes it in the same way and in the same instantaneous flash – the fraction of a second when the shutter is opened and the light-rays penetrate and reach the film. Whether one wishes to photograph the cover of a book with only its title on it, or a full page covered with fine print, it is done in the same way, takes the same length of time and produces the same result.

If, on the other hand, one wants to make a drawing this is either easy or difficult according to the subject selected. The time required to reproduce a face in profile differs greatly from that required to draw a full figure or, still more, a group of people or a landscape. A drawing, furthermore, never reproduces all the details even when we want it to do so. So much so that if a reliable document regarding a subject or the position of a body is required, a photograph and not a drawing is demanded. In the same way, to copy the title of a book is easy enough and can be done quickly but this is not the case in copying a closely-written page and as the hand works on the object the progress made shows evidence of fatigue and of the successive efforts used. But the camera, after the picture is taken, remains as before and does not show anything of what happened. To obtain the picture, the film must be taken out in a dark place, it must be exposed to chemical agents which fix the image independently of the light which produced it. Once the image is fixed, the film can be washed and exposed to light, because the image remains indelible and reproduces in all its details the object that was photographed.

It seems as if the absorbent mind acts in a like manner. There too the images must remain hidden in the darkness of the unconscious and have to be fixed by mysterious sensitivities whilst nothing yet appears outside. Only after this miraculous phenomenon has been accomplished will the creative acquisition be brought into the light of consciousness and there it remains indelible in all its particulars. In the case of language we witness an explosion shortly after two years of age, when the particular sounds, the prefixes and suffixes of words, their declination, the conjugation of the verbs and the syntactical construction of the sentence are all there. This is then the indelible mother-tongue which has become a racial characteristic.

This absorbent mind is indeed a marvellous gift to humanity!

By merely "living" and without any conscious effort the individual absorbs from the environment even a complex cultural achievement like language. If this essential mental form existed in the adult, how much easier would our studies be! Let us imagine that we could go to another world, e.g. the planet Jupiter, and that we would find men there who by merely walking about and living absorbed all the sciences without any obvious exercises. We would surely exclaim: "How great and fortunate a miracle!" Well, this fantastic mental form does exist. The mind of the young child shows this phenomenon which has remained hidden in the mysteries of the creative unconscious.

If this happens in the case of language, the construction of sounds fashioned by man during centuries of intellectual efforts to chisel the expression of thought – it is easy to acknowlede that in a similar way the other characteristics which differentiate one race from another must be fixed in the child. These are habits and customs, prejudices and feelings and generally all those characteristics which we feel to be incarnate within ourselves – features that are part of us independently, and even in spite of changes which our intelligence, logic and reason might be desirous of bringing about. I remember Gandhi once saying: "I could approve of and follow many customs of Western people, but I could never cancel from my soul the worship of the cow". How many may think "Yes, my religion appears absurd according to logic, but there remains in me, and in spite of me, a mysterious feeling of devotion towards objects – a need to have recourse to them in order to live". Those people who have grown up with the impression of their taboos cannot wipe them out even when they become doctors of philosophy. The child really builds up something. He reproduces in himself, as by a form of psychic mimesis, the characteristics of the people in his environment. Thus while growing up, he does not merely become a *man* – he becomes a *man of his race*.

With this description we have touched a psychic secret of vital importance to humanity, the secret of *adaptation* ...

1938 (2) ... The Dutch scholar De Vries discovered periods of sensitivity in animals, and we have succeeded in our schools in identifying the same "sensitive periods" in the development of children as well, and in utilizing them for the purposes of education.

KEYS TO THE WORLD

What this involves is special sensitivities that appear during the development, i.e the during the infancy of living creatures. They are of short duration and serve only to enable the acquisition of a specific ability. As soon as this has happened, the relevant sensitivity diminishes again. Thus each characteristic develops with the help of an impulse, and for a strictly limited period of time only. Growth is not a vague or inherited development, inborn in the creature, but the result of an inner process which is carefully directed by instincts which emerge at given periods, and which compel the creature at certain stages of its development to employ a level of energy that is often radically different from that of the adult individual. De Vries first identified these sensitive periods in those insects whose development is divided into particularly obvious periods, and which undergo metamorphoses that are easily accessible to experimental observation in the laboratory.

Consider the example cited by De Vries of the humble little worm, as the caterpillar of a common butterfly appears. It is known that caterpillars grow very quickly and eat voraciously, and are thus garden pests. Well, De Vries referred to a species of caterpillar which in the first days of its life is able to feed not on the large leaves of trees, but only on the very delicate little leaves that grow on the tips of branches.

But the butterfly lays its eggs at the exact opposite spot, i.e. at the point where the bough projects from the tree-trunk, in a safe and sheltered place. But who is to tell the young caterpillars, which have only just emerged from the egg, that the delicate leaves they require to eat are located out at the farthest extremities of the branches? Now, the caterpillar is endowed with a great sensitivity to light. The light attracts and fascinates it. So the young caterpillar, with its characteristic jerky movements, heads straight towards the strongest light, until it has reached the tip of the branch, where it finds the soft leaves to satisfy its hunger. The strangest thing, however, is that immediately this period is over and it has other ways of feeding, the caterpillar loses its sensitivity to light, which soon ceases to have any effect on it.

The instinct disappears. It has served its purpose, and the caterpillar now turns to other methods and sources of food.

It is not the case that the caterpillar has become insensitive to light, and therefore blind in the physical sense, but it now just ignores it.

A second period involving a different kind of sensitivity puts the butterfly larvae, which have just been greedily consuming all the surrounding plants, onto a form of starvation diet. During their period of fasting, they build themselves a coffin-like structure in which they bury themselves as if they were dead. Once again this involves an intense and inescapable labour, for it is in this grave that the final stage, the butterfly in all its winged beauty, is being prepared.

It is well-known that the larvae of bees pass through a stage in which any one, if it is a female, can become a queen. But the community chooses a single one of these larvae, and for it alone do the worker bees produce a special form of food that zoologists call "royal jelly". Thus the chosen bee, by partaking of the royal food, becomes the queen of the community. Should the bee colony want to make another larva queen after a certain period, that would not now be possible, for the period of great hunger has already passed and the larval body no longer has the capacity to develop.

This opens the way to understanding something which is of decisive importance as far as the human creature is concerned: We are dealing on the one hand with an inner impulse that gives rise to the most admirable results, and on the other with a periodic indifference that leads to blindness and unproductiveness.

The adult is unable to exert any type of external influence on these fundamental stages of development.

But if the child has not had the chance to act in accordance with his inner directives during the periods of sensitivity, then he has missed the opportunity to acquire a particular ability naturally; and this opportunity has gone for ever ...

... The child makes his acquisitions in his periods of sensitivity. These are comparable to a searchlight which sheds bright light on a certain inner sphere, or perhaps even to an electrically charged state. On the basis of this sensitivity, the child is able to establish an extraordinarily intense relationship between himself and the outside world, and from this moment on he finds everything easy, inspiring, alive. He becomes more powerful with every effort. Only when the relevant ability has been gained during such a period of sensitivity does the veil of indifference and weariness fall across his soul.

However, hardly has one of these passions of his soul died down than other flames ignite, and thus the child progresses from one conquest to the next, in an incessant pulsation of vitality which we are all familiar with under the name of the "joy and happiness of childhood". In this glorious mental flame, which burns without consuming, takes place the act of creation of the spiritual man. If, however, the period of sensitivity has passed, then further achievements can only be made through acts of reflexion and will-power, and with great difficulty and effort. And amid the inertia, the task becomes wearisome. This is the fundamental, essential difference between the psychology of the child and that of the adult, i.e. there is a special inner vitality which explains the wonderful natural achievements of the child. But should the child encounter an obstacle to his efforts during a period of sensitivity, then a type of breakdown, a deformation, occurs in his soul. The result is a spiritual ordeal about which we understand next to nothing, though almost everyone bears its scars without knowing it …

1949 (3) And how does all this happen? We say: "The child remembers things", but in order to remember something, it is necessary to have a memory, and this the child has not. On the contrary, he has to construct it. Before one can appreciate how the ordering of words in a sentence affects its meaning, one must be able to reason. But this is also a power which the child has to make.

Our mind, as it is, would not be able to do what the child's mind does. To develop a language from nothing needs a different type of mentality. This the child has. His intelligence is not of the same kind as ours.

It may be said that we acquire knowledge by using our minds; but the child absorbs knowledge directly into his psychic life. Simply by continuing to live, the child learns to speak his native tongue. A kind of mental chemistry goes on within him. We, by contrast, are recipients. Impressions pour into us and we store them in our minds; but we ourselves remain apart from them, just as a vase keeps separate from the water it contains. Instead, the child undergoes a transformation. Impressions do not merely enter his mind; they form it. They incarnate themselves in him. The child creates his own "mental flesh", using for this what he finds in the world about him. We have named this type of mentality, *The Absorbent Mind*.

For us, it is very difficult to conceive of the infant's mental power, but there can be no doubt how privileged it is. How wonderful it would be if we could retain the prodigious capacity we had as children, of romping happily, jumping and playing while learning at the same time the whole of a new language in all its intricacy! How marvellous if all knowledge came into our minds simply as a result of living, without any need for more effort than is required to eat or breathe! At first, we should notice no particular change. Then, suddenly, the things we had learned would all appear in our minds like shining stars of knowledge. We should begin to realize they were there, become conscious of ideas that had unwittingly become ours.

Supposing I said there was a planet without schools or teachers, where study was unknown, and yet the inhabitants – doing nothing but live and walk about – came to know all things, to carry in their minds the whole of learning; would you not think I was romancing? Well, just this, which seems so fanciful as to be nothing but the invention of a fertile imagination, is a reality. It is the child's way of learning. This is the path he follows. He learns everything without knowing he is learning it, and in doing so he passes little by little from the unconscious to the conscious, treading always in the paths of joy and love.

Human consciousness seems to us a great thing; to be aware of our knowledge; to have the human form of mind. But we have to pay for this, for no sooner do we become conscious than every fresh piece of knowledge costs us effort and hard work.

Sources: (1) *The Formation of Man*, p. 61–64; (2) *Kinder sind anders*, p. 61–65; (3) *The Absorbent Mind*, p. 23–24.

3. Freedom and Commitment: The "Prepared Environment"

1938 (1) As if through a spy-hole, we may look into a child's developing inner life during his period of sensitivity. We then see, as it were, the inner organs of this life at work, giving rise to psychic growth. It becomes apparent that this mental development is not random, and does not result from external influences, but from the change of sensitivities, i.e. from temporary instincts which are associated with the acquisition of different abilities. Though the environment does furnish the material in this process, it has no constructive power of its own. It merely provides the necessary means, similar to the vital substances that the body absorbs from outside through digestion and breathing.

The inner sensitivity determines what is to be absorbed at each point from the diverse environment, and which situations are most favourable to the relevant stage of development. It is this sensitivity which causes the child to pay attention to certain things and not to others. As soon as such sensitivity becomes active in the child's mind, it is as though a ray of light emanates from within which only illuminates certain objects, but leaves others in the dark. The child's entire perceptual universe then suddenly becomes restricted to this one brightly illuminated sphere. It is not just that the child now feels a strong need to place himself in certain situations and to have certain objects around him. He also develops a special, indeed unique ability to make use of these factors in his inner growth. During such periods of sensitivity, he learns, for instance, to find his way around

67

his environment, or to gain very precise control over his motor muscle system.

Here, in these sense-relations between the child and his environment, lies the key to the mysterious recess in which the marvellous growth of the spiritual embryo takes place.

We may envisage this magnificent creative activity as a succession of powerful emotions surfacing from the unconscious mind, which bring about the formation of human consciousness on coming into contact with the environment. The path they follow leads from uncertainty via certainty to activity, as we can easily observe from the example of language acquisition.

At first, the noises that reach the child from his environment form a confused, incomprehensible disorder. But then all at once the child is drawn and captivated by precisely those sounds of the articulate language which he is still unable to understand. His mind, which is still empty of thought, listens to them as to music, and becomes filled with them.

It is like an electric shock passing through the child's muscles – not through all of them, but only through those which have previously caused nothing but inarticulate screams. These groups of muscles now suddenly become active and begin to move in a regular and disciplined manner, and their newly acquired orderly action is accompanied by a change in the sounds they produce. This will have far-reaching consequences for the future of the spiritual embryo, but the child lives only for the present, on which all his concentration is focused. He is still unaware of the glorious achievements that lie ahead of him.

His ear begins to distinguish sounds, his tongue is animated by new movements. This tongue, which until now has been used only for sucking, is irresistibly compelled to seek contact with the throat, the lips and the cheeks. None of this as yet seems to have any purpose, to be of any use. The child performs these movements only because in so doing he experiences an ineffable feeling of bliss.

He expresses this innate feeling with his whole body, when he sits there with tensed limbs, clenched fists and raised head, and fixes his eyes on the moving lips of the speaking adult.

Every period of sensitivity thus seems to correspond to a divine aura which brings dead matter to life by way of the mind.

A drama is being played out inside the child, a drama of love. It represents the only great truth of the child's inner life, and provides it with total fulfilment. Yet this great constructive activity in the child, which leaves behind indelible traces and predetermines the future life of the man, takes place in humble silence.

Everything happens quietly and unnoticed, as long as conditions in the world around are sufficient to meet the child's inner needs. Consider again the case of language, that most difficult of the child's achievements, which also coincides with his most important period of sensitivity. Here, all the child's preparation remains obscure, for he is always surrounded by people who are talking, and who in so doing provide him with the material to develop his linguistic ability. The only outwardly recognizable sign of the onset of the sensitive period for language is the child's smile, his obvious joy when he hears clear and recognizable short words, or when an adult sings him the same lullaby at bedtime. The child then leaves his conscious world in a state of blessed peace and drifts across to the tranquil world of dreams. We are well aware of this, and so we bestow terms of affection on him in order to elicit his bright smile in return. And so from time immemorial parents have paid an evening visit to the bedside of their child, who craves words and music as avidly as a dying man craves comfort.

These are as it were the positive signs that a period of sensitivity is beginning. But there are also other, far more conspicuous signs of a negative kind, which appear when an obstacle in the environment stands in the way of the inner process. The presence of a period of sensitivity can then lead to violent eruptions and a form of despondency which, because we consider them to be without reason, we call moods. Moods are the expression of an emotional disorder, an unsatisfied need that gives rise to a state of tension. It represents an attempt by the soul to demand what is due to it, and to defend itself against a state it is unable to endure ...

1938 (2) ... The progressive foundation of development and growth lies in the creation of ever more intimate relations between the individual and his environment. For the formation of individuality, or what we call the freedom of the child, can only involve increasing independence from the adult, realized through an environment suited to the child, in which he can find what he requires to develop his own functions. All this is as clear and simple as saying, for instance, that a child is weaned by changing his diet to semi-solids and fruit juices, i.e. by replacing the mother's milk by the products of the environment.

The mistake which has been repeatedly made in education when envisaging the liberation of the child has been to think that this can be achieved through a hypothetical independence from the adult, and to disregard the appropriate preparation of the environment. The latter requires a branch of scientific pedagogy somewhat comparable to the study of specific rules of hygiene in the field of infant nutrition. And yet the inner preparation of the environment as the starting point for a new type of education is already so clearly and distinctly foreshadowed in its essential principles by the child himself that it could easily be achieved in practice ...

1909 (3) *The prepared environment in the Children's House*

There is only one basis for observation: the children must be free to express themselves and thus reveal those needs and attitudes which would otherwise remain hidden or repressed in an environment that did not permit them to act spontaneously. An observer obviously needs something to observe, and if he must be trained in order to be able to see and recognize objective truth, he must also have at his disposal children placed in such an environment that they can manifest their natural traits.

It was this part of the problem, which had not as yet been taken up by educators, that seemed to me to be most important and most pertinent to teaching since it has direct reference to a child's vital activities.

I therefore began by having school equipment made proportionate to the size of the children that satisfied the need they had of moving about intelligently.

The tables which I had made were of various shapes. They were strong but extremely light so that two four-year-olds could easily move them about. The chairs were light but attractive, some with seats of wood, others of straw. These were not miniature copies of adult chairs but were proportioned to a child's body. In addition to these I ordered little wooden armchairs with wide arms and others made of wicker. Small square tables for one child to sit at were also provided, and others of different sizes and shapes. These were covered with small tablecloths and decorated with vases containing flowers or plants. Part of the equipment consisted of a very low washstand that could be used by a child of three or four. The flat sides for holding soap, brushes, and towels were white and easily cleaned. The cupboards were low, light and very simple. Some were closed by a simple curtain, others had doors, each of which was locked with a different key. The safety lock was within reach of a child's hand so that he could open and shut it and place objects on the shelves. On the long narrow top of the cupboard was placed a bowl with live fish in it or other types of ornament. All around the walls, and low enough to be reached by little children, were arranged blackboards and small pictures representing pleasant family scenes or natural objects such as animals or flowers. Or there were historical or sacred pictures which could be changed from day to day.

A large coloured picture of Raphael's Madonna of the Chair was then enthroned on a wall. We have chosen this painting as the symbol and emblem of the Children's Houses. As a matter of fact these houses represent not only an advance in society but also in humanity. They are closely connected with the elevation of motherhood, the advancement of women, and the protection of posterity. Raphael's idealized Madonna of the Virgin Mother with her adorable child is not only sweet and beautiful, but next to this perfect symbol of motherhood stands the figure of John the Baptist as a beautiful young child at the beginning of that rigorous life which was to prepare the way for Christ. It is the work of the greatest Italian artist, and if one day the Children's Houses become spread throughout the world, Raphael's picture will be there to speak eloquently of the country of their origin.

The children cannot understand the symbolic meaning of the Madonna of the Chair, but they see in it something greater than in the other pictures of mothers, fathers, grand-parents, and infants, and they will enfold it in their hearts in simple piety. So much for the environment.

Practical observations.

We may begin with the first objection that rises up in the minds of those who follow the old rigid systems: as they move about, the children will upset tables and chairs and thus create noise and confusion. But such an attitude is really the result of prejudice. People have also believed that they should wrap newly born children in swaddling bands and that children who are learning to toddle about should be shut up in walkers. We still believe that there should be heavy desks in school practically nailed to the floor. All of this is based on the conviction that children should grow up immobile and that education should depend upon a child retaining a special position.

The light and easily moved tables, chairs, and armchairs permit a child to choose the most convenient position. He can make himself comfortable rather than sit in his place, and this is at once an indication of his inner freedom and a further means of education. If a child's awkward movements make a chair fall over with a crash, he has an obvious proof of his own incapacity. A similar movement among desks would have passed unnoticed. A child thus has a means of correcting himself, and when he has done so he has proof positive of it: the chairs and tables remain silent and unmoved where they are. When this happens one can say that a child has learned how to move about. On the other hand, the exact opposite was attained under the old systems. The silence and immobility of the child himself was taken as a proof of discipline. But silence and immobility of this type actually keep a child from learning how to move about with ease and grace. The result is that when he finds himself in a place where there are no desks he starts knocking over light objects. But in our schools a child learns how to behave and how to move about with ease, and this will be useful for him outside the school as well. Even though he is still a child, he knows how to act freely and correctly.

The teacher in the Children's House in Milan had a long shelf built next to a window on which were set out the containers of metal insets used in the first drawing lessons. (This material will be discussed later.) But the ledge, since it was too narrow, was awkward to use. When the children took pieces out of the containers they often sent one of them crashing to the floor, and this caused a great deal of noise as the metal pieces scattered about. The teacher decided to have the shelf altered, but the carpenter was slow in coming. In the meantime the children learned to lift the objects so carefully that the containers ceased to fall despite their precarious position.

The skill which the children had acquired in moving the objects counteracted the inadequacy of the place for keeping the equipment.

The simplicity or imperfection of external objects can therefore help in the development of a child's activity and dexterity.

All this is logical and simple, and now that it has been expounded and proved by experiments, it seems as obvious to all as the egg of Christopher Columbus.

BASIC IDEAS OF MONTESSORI'S EDUCATIONAL THEORY

Discipline and Liberty

Here is another easy objection raised by the followers of the common schools. How can one attain discipline in a class where the children are free to move about?

In our system we obviously have a different concept of discipline. The discipline that we are looking for is active. We do not believe that one is disciplined only when he is artificially made as silent as a mute and as motionless as a paralytic. Such a one is not disciplined but annihilated.

We claim that an individual is disciplined when he is the master of himself and when he can, as a consequence, control himself when he must follow a rule of life. Such a concept of active discipline is not easy to understand nor to attain. But it certainly embodies a lofty principle of education that is quite different from the absolute and undiscussed coercion that produces immobility.

A teacher must possess a special technique in order to be able to lead a child along this way of discipline, which he should follow all his life as he constantly perfects himself in it. Just as the child, when he learns to move about instead of remaining fixed in one spot, is preparing himself not for school but for a well-ordered life, so he becomes accustomed to a discipline which is not limited to the school but which extends out into society.

A child's liberty should have as its limit the interests of the group to which he belongs. Its form should consist of what we call good breeding and behaviour. We should therefore prevent a child from doing anything which may offend or hurt others, or which is impolite or unbecoming. But everything else, every act that can be useful in any way whatever, may be expressed. It should not only be permitted but it should also be observed by the teacher. This is essential. From his scientific training, a teacher should acquire not only an ability but also an interest in observing natural phenomena. In our system he should be much more passive than active, and his passivity should be compounded of an anxious scientific curiosity and a respect for the phenomena which he wishes to observe. It is imperative that a teacher understand and appreciate his position as an observer.

Such an attitude should certainly be found in a school for little children who are making the first revelations of their psychic lives. We cannot know the consequences of suppressing a child's spontaneity when he is just beginning to be active. We may even suffocate life itself. That humanity which is revealed in all its intellectual splendour during the sweet and tender age of childhood should be respected with a kind of religious veneration. It is like the sun which appears at dawn or a flower just beginning to bloom. Education cannot be effective unless it helps a child to open up himself to life.

In order to achieve this it is essential that a child's spontaneous movements should not be checked or that he be compelled to act according to the will of another. But he should not, of course, be allowed to indulge in useless or harmful activities. These must be checked and repressed.

1921 (4) The "Children's Home" is the environment that is created for the child to enable him to develop his abilities. This kind of school is not of any fixed type, but can be adapted to the means available and the prevailing external circumstances. It should be a real home, i.e. a house, viz. a group of connected rooms with a garden where the children are in control. A garden with some means of protection against the weather is ideal, because the children can play or sleep beneath the porches, as well as taking out their tables and working or eating outside. In this way, they can stay out in the fresh air almost the whole time, while being protected against the rain and the glare of the sun.

The main, middle room of the building, which is often also the only one available to the children, is the one set aside for "brain work". To this main room can be added other smaller rooms, depending on the means available and the local circumstances, for example a bathroom, a dining room, a small parlour or living room, a handicraft room, a gymnasium and a bedroom.

The equipment in these homes is unusual in that it caters for the needs of the children, not those of adults. They not only contain teaching materials that are especially relevant to the child's mental development, but also everything required to furnish this little family household. The furniture is so light that the children can handle it, and is brightly painted, so that the children can wash it with soap and water. There are small tables of various shapes and sizes: square, rectangular and round, large and small. The rectangular, elongated shape is most common, because two or more children can work at it at the same time. There are small wooden chairs for sitting, but also small wicker armchairs and sofas.

In the study, two pieces of furniture are indispensable. One is a very long cupboard with large doors. It is very low, so that a small child can place small objects on it such as vases with flowers etc. This cupboard contains the teaching materials, which belong jointly to all the children.

The other item is a tallboy with two or three rows of small drawers, each of which has a light-coloured handle (or a coloured one that stands out against its background) and a small card bearing a name. Every child has his own drawer where he puts the things that belong to him.

All around the walls hang blackboards, which are low enough to allow the children to write or draw on them, as well as nice, artistic pictures which are changed from time to time as appropriate. The pictures show children, families, landscapes, flowers and fruits, and occasionally events from the Bible and from history. There should always be ornamental and flowering plants in the room where children are working.

The study furniture also includes pieces of carpet of various colours – red, blue, pink, green and brown. The children spread out these pieces on the ground, sit on them and work with the teaching materials. Such a room is larger than normal school rooms, not only because the small tables and special chairs require more space, but also because a large part of the floor must remain unoccupied so that the children can spread out their carpets and work on them.

In the assembly room or parlour, where the children go to talk, or pass the time playing, performing music or whatever, the furniture should be particularly elaborate. There should be plenty of small tables of various kinds, small armchairs and sofas. And on the walls there should be brackets and stands of every shape and size with small statues, ornate vases or framed photographs. But above all every child should have a small flowerpot in which it can sow, tend and grow an indoor plant. On the tables, there should be large albums with colourful pictures, as well as puzzles or various geometric shapes for the children to play with just as they like, assemble figures etc. A piano, or better still other musical instruments, perhaps a child's harp, complete the furniture. In this "recreation room", the teacher can occasionally tell the children stories, which will attract a circle of eager listeners.

In addition to the tables, the dining room furniture includes low cupboards in which the children themselves can put away and fetch the crockery, the knives, forks and spoons, the table cloth and the napkins. The plates are always made of china, and the bottles and tumblers of glass. Knives are always part of the tableware.

The cloakroom. Here every child has a small wardrobe, or part of a wardrobe, to himself. In the middle of the room there are very simple wash-stands with small bowls, soap and a nailbrush. On the wall there are small wash-basins with taps, where the children fetch and pour away their water. No limits need be set on furnishing the "Children's Homes", for the children take care of everything themselves. They sweep the rooms, dust and wash the equipment, polish the metalwork, lay and clear the table, wash the dishes, sweep and roll up the carpets, do light washing and cook here. As far as their own clothes are concerned, the children get dressed and undressed without any help. They hang their clothes on little hooks which are low enough for a small child to reach, or in the case of things like their little aprons which they treat very carefully, they fold them up and put them away in the designated linen cupboard ...

1923 (5) ... But if we prepare in a "Children's House" an environment for the child that conformed to his size, to his energy and to his psychic faculties, the child would be at liberty and a great step would have been taken toward the resolution of the educational problem – the child would have his own environment.

The objects surrounding the child should in addition look solid and attractive to him, and the "house of the child" should be lovely and pleasant in all its particulars; for beauty in the school invites activity and work, as adults know that domestic beauty nourishes domestic unity. It is almost possible to say that there is a mathematical relationship between the beauty of his surroundings and the activity of the child: he will for instance be much keener to sweep with a nice broom than with an ugly one.

Children intuitively recognize these things very well by themselves. A litle girl from one of our schools in San Francisco went one day to visit a state school and immediately noticed that the desks were dusty. She said to the teacher, "Do you know why your children don't dust and instead leave everything in a mess? Because they don't have pretty dustcloths. I wouldn't want to clean without them".

The furnishings that the child will use must be washable. The motive for this is not just a hygienic one; the real reason is that washable furniture supplies the occasion for the kind of work children do very willingly. They learn to pay attention, wash off the marks and in time become habituated to being responsible for cleaning everything around them.

People always tell me to put rubber stops under the legs of furniture to lessen the noise; I prefer the noise because it signals any abrupt motion. Children do not move in a very orderly fashion and they do not know how to control their movements very well; in contrast to ours, their muscles produce disordered movement precisely because they have not yet learned physical order and economy.

In the "house of the child" every mistake, every clumsy motion reveals itself by the noise of the chair and the table, and the child will say to himself, "that's not right". There must also be a certain number of fragile objects – glasses, plates, vases and so forth. Now certainly adults will exclaim, "How come? Put glasses in the hands of three- and four-year-old children! They will surely break them!" By this comment they place more importance on the glass than on the child; an object worth a few cents seems more precious than the physical training of their children.

In a house that is truly his, a child tends to be as well behaved as possible and seeks to control his movements; in this fashion, he starts on the road to perfection without being aware of the fact …

1923 (6) The child is not merely a little animal to feed, but from the time of his birth, a creature with a spirit. If we must look after his welfare, then it is not enough to content ourselves with his physical needs: we must open the way for his spiritual development. We must, from the very first day, respect the impulses of his spirit and know how to support them.

1916 (7) (The prepared environment at school). Not only must the teacher be transformed, but the school environment must be changed. The introduction of the "material of development" into an ordinary school cannot constitute the entire external renovation. The school should become the place where the child may live in freedom, and this freedom must not be solely the intimate, spiritual liberty of internal growth. The entire organism of the child, from his physiological, vegetative part to his motor activity, ought to find in school "the best conditions for development". This includes all that physical hygiene has already put forward as aids to the life of the child. No place would be better adapted than these schools to establish and popularize reform in the clothing of children, which should meet the requirements of cleanliness and of a simplicity facilitating freedom of movement, while it should be so made as to enable children to dress themselves.

No better place could be found to carry out and popularize infant hygiene in its relation to nutrition. It would be a work of social regeneration to convince the public of the economy they might effect by such practices, to show them that elegance and propriety in themselves cost nothing – nay, more, that they demand simplicity and moderation, and therefore exclude all that superfluity which is so expensive.

The above applies more especially to schools which, like the original Children's Houses, might be instituted in the very buildings inhabited by the parents of the pupils.

Certain special requirements must be recognized in the rooms of a free school: psychical hygiene must play its part here as physical hygiene has already done. The great increase in the dimensions of modern class-rooms was dictated by physical hygiene; the ambient air space is measured by "cubature'" in relation to the physical needs of respiration; and for the same reasons, lavatories were multiplied, and bathrooms were installed; physical hygiene further decreed the introduction of concrete floors and washable dadoes, of central heating, and in many cases of meals, while gardens or broad terraces are already looked upon as essentials for the physical well-being of the child. Wide windows already admit the light freely, and gymnasia with spacious halls and a variety of complex and costly apparatus were established. Finally, the most complicated desks, sometimes veritable machines of wood and iron, with foot-rests, seats and desks revolving automatically, in order to preclude alike the movements of the child and the distortions arising from immobility, are the economically disastrous contribution of a false principle of "school-hygiene". In the modern school, the uniform whiteness and the washable quality of every object denote the triumph of an epoch in which the campaign against microbes would seem to be the sole key to human life.

Psychical hygiene now presents itself on the threshold of the school with its new precepts, precepts which economically are certainly no more onerous than those entailed by the first triumphant entry of physical hygiene.

They require, however, that schoolrooms be enlarged, not in deference to the laws of respiration, for central heating, which makes it possible to keep windows open, renders calculations based on cubic measure negligible; but because space is necessary for the liberty of movement which should be allowed to the child. However, as the child's walking exercise will not be taken indoors, this increase of space will be sufficient if it permits free movement among the furniture. Still, if an ideal perfection is to be achieved, we may say that the "psychical" class-room should be twice as large as the "physical" class-room. We all know the sense of comfort of which we are conscious when a good half of the floor space in a room is unencumbered; this seems to offer us the agreeable possibility of *moving about freely*. This sensation of well-being is more intimate than the possibility of breathing offered to us in a room of medium size crowded with furniture.

Scantiness of furniture is certainly a powerful factor in hygiene; here physical and psychical hygiene are at one. In our schools we recommend the use of "light" furniture, which is correspondingly simple and economical in the extreme. If it be washable, so much the better, especially as the children will then "learn to wash it", thus performing a pleasing and very instructive exercise. But what is above all essential is, that it should be "artistically beautiful". In this case beauty is not produced by superfluity or luxury, but by grace and harmony of the line and colour, combined with that absolute simplicity necessitated by the lightness of the furniture. Just as the modern dress of children is more elegant than that of the past, and at the same time infinitely simpler and more economical, so is this furniture.

In a "Children's House" in the country, at Palidano, built to commemorate the Marchese Carlo Guerrieri Gonzaga, we initiated the study of "artistic" furnishing. It is well known that every little corner of Italy is a storehouse of local art, and there is no province which in bygone times did not contain graceful and convenient objects, due to a combination of practical sense and artistic instinct. Nearly all these

81

treasures are now being dispersed, and the very memory of them is dying out, under the tyranny of the stupid and uniform "hygienic" fashions of our day. It was therefore a delightful undertaking on the part of Maria Maraini to make careful inquiries into the local rustic art of the past, and to give it new life by reproducing, in the furniture of the "Children's Houses", the forms and colours of tables, chairs, sideboards and pottery, the designs of textiles and the characteristic decorative motives to be met with in old country-houses. This revival of rustic art will bring back into use objects used by the poor in ages less wealthy than ours, and meanwhile may be a revelation in "economy". If, instead of school benches, such simple and graceful objects were manufactured, even this school furniture would show how beauty may be evolved from ugliness by eliminating superfluous material; for beauty is a question, not of material, but of inspiration. Hence we must not look to richness of material, but to refinement of spirit for these practical reforms.

If similar studies should be made some day upon the rustic art of all the Italian provinces, each of which has its special artistic traditions, "types of furniture" might arise which would in themselves do much to elevate the taste and refine the habits. They would bring to the enlightenment of the world an "educational mode", because this time-honoured artistic feeling of a people with a very ancient civilization would breathe new life into those moderns who seem to be suffocating under the obsession of physical hygiene, and to be actuated solely by a despairing effort to combat disease.

We should witness the humanization of art, rising amidst the ugliness and darkness of those who have accustomed themselves to think only of death. Indeed, the "hygienic houses" of today with their bare walls and white washable furniture, look like hospitals; while the schools seem veritable tombs, with their desks ranged in rows like black catafalques – black, merely because they have to be of the same colour as ink to hide the stains which are looked upon as a necessity, just as certain sins and certain crimes are still considered to be inevitable in the world; the alternative of avoiding them has never occurred to any one.

Class-rooms have black desks, and bare, grey walls, more devoid of ornament than those of a mortuary chamber; this is to the end that the starved and famishing spirit of the child may "accept" the indigestible intellectual food which the teacher bestows upon it. In other words, every distracting element has to be removed from the environment, so that the teacher, by his oratorical art, and with the help of his laborious expedients, may succeed in fixing the rebellious attention of his pupils on himself. On the other hand, the spiritual school puts no limits to the beauty of its environment, save economical limits. No ornament can distract a child really absorbed in his task; on the contrary, beauty both promotes concentration of thought and offers refreshment to the tired spirit. Indeed, the churches, which are *par excellence* places of meditation and repose for the life of the soul, have called upon the highest inspirations of genius to gather every beauty within their precincts.

Such words may seem strange; but if we wish to keep in touch with the principles of science, we may say that the place best adapted to the life of man is an artistic environment; and that, therefore, if we want the school to become "a laboratory for the observation of human life", we must gather within it things of *beauty*, just as the laboratory of the bacteriologist must be furnished with stoves and soils for the culture of bacilli.

Furniture for children, their tables and chairs, should be light, not only that they may be easily carried about by childish arms, but because their very fragility is of educational value. The same consideration leads us to give children china plates, glass drinking-vessels and fragile ornaments, for these objects become the *denouncers* of rough, disorderly, and undisciplined movements. Thus the child is led to correct himself, and he accordingly trains himself not to knock against, overturn, and break things; softening his movements more and more, he gradually becomes their perfectly free and self-possessed director. In the same way the child will accustom himself to do his utmost *not to soil* the gay and pretty things which enliven his surroundings. Thus he makes progress in his own perfection, or in other words, it is thus he achieves the perfect co-ordination of his voluntary movements. It is the same process by which, having enjoyed silence and music, he will do all in his power to avoid discordant noises, which have become unpleasant to his educated ear.

On the other hand, when a child comes into collision a hundred times with an enormously heavy iron-bound desk, which a porter would have difficulty in moving; when he makes thousands of invisible ink-stains on a black bench; when he lets a metal plate fall to the ground a hundred times without breaking it, he remains immersed in his sea of defects without perceiving them; his environment meanwhile is so constructed as to hide and therefore to encourage his errors, with Mephistophelian hypocrisy.

Free movement

It is now a hygienic principle universally accepted that children require movement. Thus, when we speak of "free children", we generally imply that they are free to move, that is, to run and jump. No mother nowadays fails to agree with the children's doctor that her child should go into parks and meadows and move about freely in the open air.

When we talk of liberty for children in school, some such conception of physical liberty as this rises at once in the mind. We imagine the free child making perilous leaps over the desks, or dashing madly against the walls; his "liberty of movement" seems necessarily to imply the idea of "a wide space", and accordingly we suppose that, if confined to the narrow limits of a room, it would inevitably become a conflict between violence and obstacles, a disorder incompatible with discipline and work.

But in the laws of "psychical hygiene", "liberty of movement" is not limited to a conception so primitive as that of merely "animated bodily liberty". We might, indeed, say of a puppy or a kitten what we say of children: that they should be free to run and jump, and that they should be able to do so, as in fact they often do, in a park or a field, with and like the children. If, however, we wish to apply the same conception of motor liberty to our treatment of a bird, we should make certain arrangements for it; we should place within its reach the branch of a tree, or crossed sticks which would afford foothold for its claws, since these are not designed to be spread out on the ground like the feet of creeping things, but are adapted to gripping a stick. We know that a bird "left free to move" over a vast, illimitable plane would be miserable.

How, then, is it that we never think thus: if it be necessary to prepare different environments for a bird and a reptile in order to ensure their liberty of movement, must it not be a mistake to provide the same form of liberty for our children as that proper to cats and dogs? Children, indeed, when left to themselves to take exercise, show impatience, and are prone to quarrel and cry; older children feel it necessary to invent something whereby they may conceal from themselves the intolerable boredom and humiliation of walking for walking's sake, and running for running's sake. They try to find some object for their exertions; the younger children play pranks. The activity of children thus left to themselves has rarely a good result; it does not aid development, save as regards the physical advantage of general nutrition, that is, of the vegetative life. Their movements become ungraceful; they invent unseemly capers, walk with a staggering gait, fall easily and break things. They are evidently quite unlike the free kitten, so full of grace, so fascinating in its movements, tending to perfect its actions by the light jumping and running which are natural to it. In the motor instinct of the child there appears to be no grace, no natural impulse towards perfection. Hence we must conclude that the movement which suffices for the cat does not suffice for the child, and that if the nature of the child is different, his path of liberty must also be different.

If the child has no "intelligent aim" in his movements, he is without internal guidance, thus movement tires him.

BASIC IDEAS OF MONTESSORI'S EDUCATIONAL THEORY

Many men feel the dreadful emptiness of being compelled to "move without an object". One of the cruel punishments invented for the chastisement of slaves was to make them dig deep holes in the earth and fill them up again repeatedly, in other words, to make them work without an object.

Experiments on fatigue have shown that work with an intelligent object is far less fatiguing than an equal quantity of aimless work. So much so, that the psychiatrists of today recommend, not "exercise in the open air", but "work in the open air", to restore the individuality of the neurasthenic.

"Reconstructive" work – work, that is to say, which is not the product of a "mental effort", but tends to the co-ordination of the psycho-muscular organism. Such are the activities which are not directed to the *production* of objects, but to their *preservation*, as, for instance, dusting or washing a little table, sweeping the floor, laying or clearing the table, cleaning shoes, spreading out a carpet. These are the tasks performed by a servant to *preserve* the objects belonging to his master, work of a very different order to that of the artificer, who, on the other hand, *produced* those objects by an intelligent effort. The two classes of work are profoundly different. The one is simple; it is a co-ordinated activity scarcely higher in degree than the activity required for walking or jumping; for it merely gives purpose to those simple movements, whereas *productive* work entails a preliminary intellectual work of preparation, and comprises a series of very complicated motor movements, together with an application of sensory exercises.

The first is the work suitable for little children, who must "exercise themselves in order to learn to co-ordinate their movements".

It consists of the so-called exercises of practical life which correspond to the psychical principle of "liberty of movement". For this it will be sufficient to prepare "a suitable environment", just as we should place the branch of a tree in an aviary, and then to leave the children free to follow their instincts of activity and imitation. The surrounding objects should be proportioned to the size and strength of the child:

light furniture that he can carry about; low dressers within reach of his arms; locks that he can easily manipulate; drawers that open easily; light doors that he can open and shut readily; clothes-pegs fixed on the walls at a height convenient for him; brushes his little hand can grasp; pieces of soap that can lie in the hollow of such a hand; basins so small that the child is strong enough to empty them; brooms with short, smooth, light handles; clothes he can easily put on and take off himself; these are surroundings which invite activity, and among which the child will gradually perfect his movements without fatigue, acquiring human grace and dexterity, just as the little kitten acquires its graceful movement and feline dexterity solely under the guidance of instinct.

The field thus opened to the free activity of the child will enable him to exercise himself and to form himself as a man. It is not movement for its own sake that he will derive from these exercises, but a powerful coefficient in the complex formation of his personality. His social sentiments in the relations he forms with other free and active children, his collaborators in a kind of household designed to protect and aid their development; the sense of dignity acquired by the child who learns to satisfy himself in suroundings he himself preserves and dominates – these are the coefficients of humanity which accompany "liberty of movement". From his consciousness of this development of his personality the child derives the impulse to persist in these tasks, the industry to perform them, the intelligent joy he shows in their completion. In such an environment he undoubtedly *works himself*, and fortifies his spiritual being, just as when his body is bathed in fresh air and his limbs move freely in the meadow, he works at the growth of his physical organism and strengthens it.

1938 (8) ... One day, the teacher arrived late at the school. She had forgotten to lock the cupboard containing the teaching materials, and she found that the children had opened it and were crowding round. Some of them had picked up certain objects and had taken them away, behaviour which the teacher took to indicate thievish instincts. She thought that children who took things away, and lacked respect for the school and the teacher, ought to be dealt with strictly and taught right from wrong. My own interpretation of the matter, however, was that the children were already sufficiently familiar with these objects to be able to make their own choice from among them. And this was in fact the case.

This was the start of some lively and interesting activity. The children revealed various preferences, and chose what to do accordingly. Since then, we have switched to using the low cupboards, in which the material is within the children's reach and freely available, so that they may choose it themselves on the basis of their own inner needs. Thus, to the principle of repetition of the exercises was added the further principle of free choice, something which gave rise to to all kinds of observations concerning the children's inclinations and inner needs.

One of the first interesting results was that the children were not interested in all of the material I had prepared, but only in individual items. They more or less all made the same choices. There was an obvious preference for some objects, while others remained untouched and gradually gathered dust.

I showed the children all of the material, and made sure that the teacher accurately explained to them the use of each item, but they chose not to return to certain objects.

In time I came to realize that *everything* in the child's environment not only requires order, but *must also be carefully measured*, and that interest and concentration increase as confusion and superfluity are eliminated.

1916 (9) It is therefore necessary that the environment should contain the means of auto-education. These means cannot be "taken at random"; they represent the result of an experimental study which cannot be undertaken by all, because a scientific preparation is necessary for such delicate work; besides, like all experimental study, it is laborious, prolonged, and exact. Many years of research are required before the means really *necessary* for *psychical development* can be set forth. Those educationalists who leave the great question of the liberty of the pupil to the good sense or to the preparation of the master are very far from solving the problem of liberty. The greatest scientist or the person most fitted by nature to teach, could never of himself discover such, because, to preparation and natural gifts, the further factor of *time* must be added – the long period of preparatory experiment. Therefore a *science* which has already *provided the means* for self-education must exist beforehand. Today, he who speaks of liberty in the schools ought at the same time to exhibit objects – approximating to a scientific apparatus – which will make such liberty possible.

Sources: (1) *Kinder sind anders*, p. 66–69; (2) *Ibid.*, p. 258; (3) *The Discovery of the Child*, p. 48–52; (4) *Mein Handbuch*, p. 8–12; (5) *Das Kind in der Familie*, p. 74–76, cf. *The Child in the Family*, p. 42–44; (6) *The Child in the Family*, p. 52–53; (7) *The Advanced Montessori Method I*, p. 111–118; (8) *Kinder sind anders*, p. 168–169; (9) *The Advanced Montessori Method I*, p. 57.

4. The Individual and the Community: "Wasted Energies"?

1916 (1) … The child is making his first trial of arms, and his personality is a very different thing from that just described. In comparison with the adult, he is an unbalanced creature, almost invariably the prey of his own impulses and sometimes subject to the most obstinate inhibitions. The two opposite activities of the will have not yet combined to form the new personality. The psychical embryo has still the two elements separate. The great essential is that this "combination", this "adaptation", should take place and establish itself as a supporting girdle at the margin of consciousness. Hence it is necessary to induce active exercise as soon as possible, since this is essential to such a degree of development. The aim in view is not to make the child a little precocious "gentleman", but to induce him to exercise his powers of volition, and to bring about as soon as possible the reciprocal contact of impulses with inhibitions. It is this "construction" itself which is necessary, not the result which may be achieved externally by means of this construction.

It is, in fact, merely a means to an end: and the end is that the child should act together with other children, and practise the gymnastics of the will in the daily habits of life. The child who is absorbed in some task, inhibits all movements which do not conduce to the accomplishment of this work; he makes a selection among the muscular co-ordinations of which he is capable, persists in them, and thus begins to make such co-ordinations permanent. This is a very different matter to the disorderly movements of a child giving way to unco-ordinated impulses. When he begins to respect the work of others; when he waits patiently for the object he desires instead of snatching it from the hand of another; when he can walk about without knocking against his companions, without stamping on their feet, without overturning the table – then he is organizing his powers of volition, and bringing impulses and inhibitions into equilibrium. Such an attitude prepares the way for the habits of social life. It would be impossible to bring about such a result by keeping children motionless, seated side by side; under such conditions "relations between children" cannot be established, and infantile social life does not develop.

It is by means of free intercourse, of real practice which obliges each one to adapt his own limits to the limits of others, that social "habits" may be established. Dissertations on what ought to be done will never bring about the construction of the will; to make a child acquire graceful movements, it will not suffice to inculcate "ideas of politeness" and of "rights and duties". If this were so, it would suffice to give a minute description of the movements of the hand necessary in playing the piano, to enable an attentive pupil to execute a sonata by Beethoven. In all such matters the "formation" is the essential factor; the powers of will are established by exercise.

1916 (2) ... Therefore the child whom his mother has loved and who was helped by that love, has that "internal sense" by means of which he is capable of love. The "human objects" which present themselves to that sense have reflections from it.

We should "wait to be seen" by him; the day will come when, among all the intellectual objects, the child will perceive our spirit and will come to us to take his ease within us. It will be to him a new birth, akin to that other awakening, when some one of the objects first attracted him and held him. It is impossible that that day, that moment, should not arrive. We have performed a delicate work of love towards the child, presenting to him the means which satisfy his intellectual needs, without making ourselves felt, keeping ourselves in the background, but always present and ready to help. We have given great satisfaction to the child by succouring him; when he needed to clarify the order of his mind still further by language, we offered him the names of things, but only these, retiring at once without asking anything from him, without putting forward anything from ourselves. We have revealed to him the sounds of the alphabet, the secret of numbers, we have put him into relation with things but restricting ourselves to what was useful to him, almost concealing our body, our breathing, our person.

When he felt a desire to choose, he never found an obstacle in us; when he occupied himself a long time with an exercise, we kept our distance, in order to protect the tranquility of his work, as a mother protects the refreshing sleep of her babe.

When he made his first plunge into abstraction, he felt nothing in us but the echo of his joy.

The child found us always indefatigable when he called upon us, almost as if our mission to him were to offer him what he requires, just as it is the mission of the flower to give perfume without limit or intermission.

He found with us a new life, no less sweet than the milk he drew from his mother's breast, with which his first love was born. Therefore he will one day become sensitive to this being who lives to make him live, from whose self-sacrifice his freedom to live and expand is derived.

And undoubtedly the day will come when his spirit will become sensitive to our spirit; and then he will begin to taste that supreme delight which lies in the intimate contact of soul with soul, and our voice will no longer be heard by his ear alone. The power to obey us, to communicate his conquests to us, to share his joys with us, will be the new element in his life. We shall see the child who suddenly becomes aware of his companions and is almost as deeply interested as we are in their progress and their work. It will be delightful to witness such a scene as that of four or five children sitting with spoons arrested over the smoking bowl, and no longer sensitive to the stimulus of hunger because they are absorbed in contemplation of the efforts of a very little companion who is trying to tuck his napkin under his chin, and finally succeeds in doing so; and then we shall see these spectators assume an expression of relief and pride, almost like that of a father who is present at the triumph of his son. Children will recompense us in the most amazing manner by their progress, their spiritual effusions and their sweet obedience. The fruit they will cause us to gather will be abundant beyond anything we can imagine. Thus it comes to pass when the secrets of life are interpreted: "Give and it shall be given unto you: good measure, pressed down and shaken together, and running over shall men give into your bosom".

1923 (3) Children from three age-groups should be brought together in the same class. This should help the youngest ones, who are naturally interested in what the older ones are doing, and can learn from them. A child who shows a desire to work and learn must have the liberty to do so, even if the work is not part of the regular syllabus, which is only necessary for the teacher beginning work with a class ...

What difference of age should there be among children in a group? Not more than three years difference. The groups should comprise children from three to six years, six to nine years, and nine to twelve years of age. I do not recommend single-age classes like those in ordinary schools. Many people think, for instance, that we put children of between three and six years of age together in one room because we have insufficient space, or an insufficient number of children for three classes. I have often been told that a school which has grown to over two hundred children has divided them into three classes, one for children aged three, one for those of four, and one for those between five and six etc.

Even if we had more than a thousand children, and a school like a palace, I would still consider it advisable to keep children with an age difference of three years together. This age difference and this mixture of different stages of development are one of the fundamentals of self-education …

1949 (4) Usually, teachers do not understand the social aspect of our work. They think that the Montessori schools encourage the curriculum subjects, but not social life. They say, "If the child works on his own, then what becomes of social life?" But what is social life if not the solving of problems, behaving properly and making plans acceptable to all? They consider social behaviour as sitting side by side and listening to the teacher, but that is certainly not social life.

If there are a large number of children in a class, differences of character show themselves in a wealth of social phenomena. This does *not* happen if only a few children are present. Indeed, the highest stages of inner development and perfection derive from these social experiences.

Consider now the composition of this society of children. These children, who have been brought together in a closed environment, are of mixed ages (between three and six). This does not occur in ordinary schools, unless the older children are backward. The children are usually grouped by age, and only rarely does one find vertical grouping in a class. But the children themselves reveal to us how difficult it is to promote the development of children of the same age, and consequently of about equal ability. A mother may have six children and yet maintain an orderly household. But if there are twins, triplets or maybe even quadruplets, then things become harder, for it is very trying to care for four children who all want the same thing at the same time. The mother with six children of different ages is better off than the mother with one. The only child is especially difficult. This is not so much because he is spoilt, but because he lacks companionship. He has a much harder time of it than other children. In families where the first child is difficult, later children often present no problems. This is put down to the fact that the parents are now more experienced, but is really because the children now have their own social environment.

Social life is interesting because it involves so many different types. A home for old men or women is something sad. It is something totally unnatural, and it is wrong to bring together people of the same age. It is also wrong to do this with children, as it breaks the bonds of social life. In many schools, separation is first by sex and then by age, with each year assigned its own class. This is a fundamental error, which leads to all kinds of problems – this artificial isolation which impedes the development of the social sense. In our schools co-education is common for young children, but is perhaps not really that important. Boys and girls could have their separate classes, but each class should contain a mixture of different ages. Our schools have shown how children of different ages help one another. The younger ones watch what the older ones are doing and ask all kinds of questions, and the older ones explain. This is really useful teaching, for the way that a five year old interprets and explains things is so much nearer than ours to the mind of a child of three that the little one learns easily, whereas we would scarcely be able to get through to him. There is a harmony and communication between them that is not possible between an adult and such a young child. Teachers are unable to convey everything to a child of three, but a five year old child explains it all. There is a natural mental osmosis between them. A child of three is also quite capable of taking an interest in the work of a five year old, because in fact the difference in their abilities is not that great. In this way the five year olds become heroes and teachers, and all the younger ones admire them greatly. The younger ones turn to the older ones for inspiration, and then set to work themselves. In ordinary schools the best pupils should also perhaps be able to teach the others, but this is not usually allowed. The only thing they may do is to give a correct answer when the others cannot, and this breeds envy. Little children are not envious, they do not feel humiliated by learning from a small friend. They simply know that they are the younger ones, and that when they are older, their turn will come. There is love and admiration here, a true brotherhood. In the old type of school, the only way of raising standards was through emulation, which means envy, hatred, disparagement and much more that is oppressive and antisocial. The intelligent child becomes vain and acquires power over others, whereas in our schools the five year old feels himself to be a protector of the three year olds. It is hard to understand fully how deep and crucial this atmosphere of protection and admiration becomes. The class becomes a group, cemented together by affection.

The children get to know one another's characters, develop very strong mutual awareness, and observe one another. In the old type of school, the only thing they knew was that "So and so has won the first prize", or "The other boy's marks are unsatisfactory".

True fellow feeling cannot establish itself in such conditions, but this is the age in which social and antisocial tendencies are going to develop in the context of the child's surroundings. This is their point of origin.

People are concerned about whether a child of five who is always helping other children will make sufficient progress himself. But, firstly, he doesn't spend his whole time teaching, but has his own freedom and knows how to use it. Secondly, teaching really allows him to consolidate and strengthen his own knowledge, which he must analyze and use anew each time, so that he comes to see everything with greater clarity. The older child also gains from this exchange.

The group for children of three to six is not even separated from that of the seven to nine year olds. Thus, children of six again get their inspiration from the group above. The walls of all our classrooms are only waist-high partitions, and there is easy access from one classroom to another, because there are many reasons why a child might want to enter another class. If a child of three enters the class of the six to nine year olds, he does not stay long, because he sees he can find nothing there of any use to him. There are thus natural demarcations, but no separation, and every class is open to the others. Each group has its own environment, but is not isolated. One can always go for an "intellectual visit" or an intellectual excursion. A child of three can therefore watch a nine year old working out a square root. He may ask him what he is doing. If the answer leaves him none the wiser, he returns to his class, but the six year old watches with interest and may learn something from it. This freedom allows us to tell the limits of understanding at each age. Thus we discovered that eight and nine year old children understood how to work out square roots, something that twelve to fourteen year olds were learning at the time. In this way we also realized that children of eight are interested in and enjoy algebra. Thus the child's progress does not depend only on his age, but also on being free to go where he wishes. There is general enthusiasm, and inferiority complexes are unknown. The younger children are full of enthusiasm because they know what the older ones are doing, the older ones because they can teach others what they know themselves. This results in an increase in spiritual energy.

All this and more goes to show that the events which seemed so extraordinary were in fact nothing other than the natural result of following natural laws.

All these energies are simply wasted in ordinary teaching, but once they cease to be squandered there will be the promise of new intellectual wealth for future generations.

Studying the behaviour of these children and their mutual relationships in an atmosphere of freedom reveals the true secrets of social life. These are facts so delicate and refined that they need to be examined under a spiritual microscope, but they are of immense importance, for they reveal their origin deep within the nature of man. That is why these schools are sometimes represented as laboratories of psychological research, although no research as such takes place, but rather observation, important observation.

Things of great value are revealed, for example that children know how to solve their own problems. If we observe children without interfering, then we notice something significant: children do not help one another in the same way as we do. We may see children carrying something heavy, but none of the others come to their aid, or nobody helps them when they are bringing back all the material for a challenging task. They respect one another, and only give help when it is really necessary. This is very useful to us, for they appear to be intuitively aware of the child's basic concern not to be helped unnecessarily, and this is something they respect. One day, a small child had spread out all the geometric cards with their figures on the floor. Suddenly, music was heard outside and a procession passed by. All the children hurried to see it, except for the little boy with all the material. He did not go, for he would not have dreamt of leaving the material lying around like that. It had to be put away, and he was used to doing this alone, but there were tears in his eyes, for he too would have liked to see the procession.

The others noticed this, and all turned back to help him. Adults lack this fine power of discrimination which allows them to know when help is needed. More often than not they help one another when it is not necessary. A man will often, in the name of good manners, draw up a chair for a young lady as she seats herself at table, though she can quite well do it for herself. Or else he will offer her his arm as she goes downstairs, though she could quite easily manage alone. But if somebody suffers a misfortune, then nobody comes to his aid. When help is required, then nobody offers it, but if it is not required then everyone helps! This is an area where children have nothing to learn from adults, who are not nearly as competent as children. I believe that in his unconscious mind, the child still retains the memory of his wish and need to make the maximum effort, and this is why he does not help others when his help might do some harm. It is also interesting to see how children deal with "disruptive pupils", for instance with a newcomer to a group who is still unfamiliar with it, causes disturbance, and is a real problem for the teacher and the children. Usually the teacher might say "That is very naughty; it isn't at all nice!", or perhaps even "You are a bad little boy!", but the children's reaction is different. One of the children approached the newcomer and said, "You are naughty, but that is not bad, listen, when we first came we were just as naughty as you". His bad behaviour was seen as a misfortune, and a child tried to comfort him and to bring out the real little boy within him. He felt sorry for him. How society would change if wrongdoers aroused our sympathy, and we were bold enough to try and comfort them, to show them the sort of sympathy we would show the sick. Wrongdoing is often psychopathologically determined, and due to a poor environment, a deprived background, or great disappointments. Sympathy and help are needed here just as much as punishment. This would change our social structure for the better.

If a mishap occurs amongst our children, for instance if a vase is smashed, the child to whom it happens is often desperate, for they don't like breaking things … , and they are normally capable of carrying a vase properly. The adult's impulsive reaction is to shout, "Just look at what you have done, you've broken it, I told you not to do that!" Or at the very least we would tell the child to pick up the pieces, for we believe he will take more note if he has to put right the consequences of his actions. But what do the children do? They all come over to help, and with a helpful tone in their little voices they say, "Well, let's get another one then". Some will pick up the pieces, another will mop up the running water on the floor. It is an instinct which leads them to help the weak, encouraging and comforting them, and this is an instinct for social progress. Indeed, there has been great social progress since mankind started to look after and help the weak.

This was the basis on which the whole science of medicine was built, with help given instinctively not only to those who arouse pity, but to the whole of mankind. It is not wrong to encourage and help the weak and the inferior. On the contrary, it is right to do so, and brings about general social progress. These are feelings which children show as soon as they have become normalized, and not only for one another, but also for animals. Isn't the general belief that children must be taught respect for animals, and that they are naturally inclined to be cruel to them? This is not true, their natural instinct is to protect animals. In our school at Kodaikanal we had a young goat, which I used to feed daily, holding the food up high so that to reach it the little creature had to stand on its hind legs. I enjoyed watching the animal do this, and it too seemed to find it fun. But one day, a child approached with an anxious look on his little face and held the goat firmly under the belly with both hands, believing that it could not stand properly on just its two hind legs. These were the sentiments of a kind little heart. Something else we see in our school is how children admire those who do better than they do.

Not only do they show no envy, but things that others do well arouse their enthusiastic admiration and joy, as happened for instance with the now famous explosion into writing. The first word to be written caused great joy and great jubilation. They looked admiringly at the writer and they too were suddenly moved to write, saying "I can do it too!" The achievement of one suddenly gave impetus to the whole group. There was the same enthusiasm for the alphabet, and one day the group made a procession using the letters as banners, and there was such joy and happy cheering that people came up from below (we were actually on a flat roof) to see the cause of all the joy. "They are so delighted at learning the alphabet", the teacher explained.

There is communication among children that rests on noble feelings, and this forms the basis of their unity. At moments like these, we realize that in the atmosphere created by an intense emotional life there is a kind of mutual attraction among normalized children. Just as the older children are drawn to the younger ones, and the younger children to the older ones, so are the normalized children drawn to those who are not normalized, and *vice versa*.

Sources: (1) *The Advanced Montessori Method I*, p. 134–135; (2) *Ibid.*, p. 256–258; (3) Joosten-Chotzen, R., *What Difference of Age should there be among Children in a Montessori-Group?*, p. 12–14; (4) *Aan de Basis van het Leven*, p. 241–248.

5. Good and Evil: The New Educator and the Child's Conscience

1921 (1) ... The old philosophical dispute about whether man is born good or evil is often raised in connection with my method, as it would be proof of the natural goodness of man. However, very many others have come out against it, on the grounds that it would be a dangerous mistake to leave children to their own devices, given their innate inclination towards evil.

I should like to provide a positive basis for this question.

By "good" and "evil", we mean very many different things, and the concepts involved are particularly vague as far as our actual attitudes towards younger children are concerned.

The tendencies which we stigmatize as evil in three to six year old children are often merely those which we adults happen to find annoying when, failing to recognize their needs, we seek to suppress their every movement, their every attempt to acquire experience of the world (by touching objects etc.). But the child directs his natural inclinations towards organizing his movements, towards forming impressions, and especially experiencing sensations, so that, when opposed, he starts to resist, and this is essentially what makes him naughty.

It is no wonder that the evil vanishes as soon as the child no longer has reason to resist, when we provide him with the proper means of development and allow him to use them in complete freedom.

And when his old tantrums give way to a series of joyful outbursts, the child's moral physiognomy gradually assumes an expression of calm and gentleness which makes him seem like a completely different being.

We have forced children into the violent manifestation of a veritable struggle for existence. In order to meet the needs of their spiritual development, they have often had to fight to secure from us the things they thought necessary. They have had to act contrary to our laws, or sometimes fight with other children for the things they desired.

On the other hand, if we give children the means they need to live, the struggle for them ceases, and its place is taken by a powerful expansion of life. This question concerns a principle of hygiene relating to the nervous system during the difficult period in which the brain is still undergoing rapid development, and should be of great interest to specialists in children's diseases and nervous conditions. The inner life of man and his intellectual development are governed by special laws and basic requirements which we must not forget if our goal is the health of the human race.

For this reason, the issue of a method of education which fosters and protects the inner activity of the child is not only of concern to schools and teachers. It is a general issue that involves the whole family, and is of prime importance to mothers!

Often the only way of answering a question correctly is to analyze it more thoroughly. Thus, if we saw some men fighting over a piece of bread, we would probably say, "Aren't men evil!" On the other hand, if we were to enter a cosy restaurant and see people sitting down quietly and choosing their meal, without any obvious ill-will between them, we might say, "Aren't men good!" Obviously, the question of absolute good and evil, our instinctive conceptions of which guide us in our superficial judgement, transcends these narrow limits. Thus, for instance, we could establish quality restaurants for an entire nation, without directly influencing its morality. To be sure, in a superficial judgement we might say that a well-nourished nation is better and more peaceful and commits less crimes than an undernourished one. But whoever concluded from this that a good diet is all it takes to make men good, would obviously be mistaken.

Yet it cannot be denied that a good diet is an essential tool for creating good, in the sense that it eliminates all misdeeds and feelings of resentment that are due to hunger.

In our case, we are concerned with a much more profound need – that of nourishing the inner life of man and his higher functions. The bread involved here is the bread of the spirit, and we are faced with the difficult task of satisfying man's spiritual needs.

We have already achieved a very interesting result when we succeeded in providing new means which allow children to attain a higher state of calm and kindness, means which we have already been able to test empirically. All our achievements are based on these means which we have discovered, and which fall into two categories: the organization of work and freedom.

The integral organization of work, which affords the opportunity for self-development and provides an outlet for energy, gives each child a pleasant and reassuring sense of satisfaction. And under the conditions in which the child works, his freedom leads him to perfect his abilities and to learn excellent discipline, which itself results from that new quality, stillness, which has developed within him.

Freedom without organization of work would be useless. Children left to themselves without the resources of work would perish, just as a baby left alone without food would perish through privation. Accordingly, the organization of work is the cornerstone of this new structure for good, but even this organization would be futile without the child being free to use it, and without an opportunity for children to develop all those powers which arise when their highest abilities are satisfied.

Is something like this not also evident in world history? The history of civilization is that of successful attempts to organize labour and achieve freedom. On the whole, man has indeed improved, as his progress from barbarism to civilization shows, and it may be said that crimes, those various manifestations of wickedness, cruelty and violence, have continually decreased over time.

The criminality of our own time has been viewed as a form of barbarism that has survived in the midst of civilized nations. Through better organization of work, society will therefore probably achieve further improvements, and in the meantime it appears quite ready to tear down the last barriers between itself and freedom.

Society shows us the sort of results we can expect from children of three to six years of age, if their work is fully organized, and their freedom is complete! This is why they appear to us as harbingers of hope and salvation.

If men, whose progress along the path of work and freedom has been so difficult and imperfect, have nevertheless improved, then why should we fear that the same path will prove disastrous for children?

On the other hand, I would not wish to claim that the goodness that our little children have achieved in their independence might resolve the question of the abolute good or evil of man. All we can say is that by removing the obstacles which are the causes of violence and insubordination, we have made a contribution to good. Thus we "render unto Caesar the things which are Caesar's, and to God the things which are God's!"

1916 (2) To keep alive and to perfect psychical sensibility is the essence of moral education. Around it, as in the intellectual education which proceeds from the exercise of the senses, *order* establishes itself: the distinction between right and wrong is perceived. No one can *teach* this distinction in all its details to one who cannot see it. But to see the difference and to know it are not the same thing.

But in order that "the child may be helped" it is essential that the environment should be rightly organized, and that good and evil should be duly differentiated. An environment where the two things are confused, where good is confounded with apathy and evil with activity, good with prosperity and evil with misfortune, is not one adapted to assist the establishment of order in the moral consciousness, much less is one where acts of flagrant injustice and persecutions occur. Under such conditions the childish consciousness will become like water which has been made turbid, and more poisonous than is alcohol to the life of the foetus. Order may perhaps be banished forever, together with the clarity of the consciousness; and we cannot tell what may be the consequences to the "moral man". "Whoever shall offend one of these little ones, it were better for him ... that he were drowned in the depth of the sea". "If thy hand or thy foot offend thee, cut it off and cast it from thee".

However, the properly organized environment is not everything. Even in intellectual education it was not the spontaneous exercise alone which refreshed the intelligence; but further, the lessons of the teacher which confirmed and illuminated the internal order in process of development. On these occasions she said: "This is red, this is green". Now she will say: "This is right, this is wrong". And it will not be unusual to find children like the one described above, who make good and evil the centre of consciousness, and, placing it above material bread and intellectual nourishment, will propound the question more vital to them than any other: "What is good? and what is evil?" But we must not forget that moral lessons should be brief; and that Moses, the father of the sages, in order to inculcate morality, not in a child but in a race, gave ten simple commandments, which to Christ seemed superfluous. It is true, however, that at the head of these was the "law" of love; and that Christ substituted for the Decalogue an amplification of that law, which comprises within itself all legislations and moral codes.

It is possible that good and evil may be distinguished by means of an "internal sense", apart from cognitions of morality; and in such a case, of course, the good and evil in question would be absolute; that is to say, they would be bound up with life itself, and not with acquired social habits. We always speak of a "voice of conscience" which teaches us from within to distinguish the two things: good confers serenity, which is order; enthusiasm, which is strength; evil is signalized as an anguish which is at times unbearable; remorse, which is not only darkness and disorder, but fever, a malady of the soul. It is certain that the laws of society, public opinion, material well-being and threats of peril would all be powerless to produce these various sensations. Often serenity is to be found among the unfortunate, whereas the remorse of Lady Macbeth, who saw the spot of blood upon her hand, gnawed at the heart of one who had acquired a kingdom.

Is it not surprising that there should be an internal sensation which warns us of perils and causes us to recognize the circumstances favourable to life. If science in these days demonstrates that the means of preserving even material life correspond to the moral "virtues", we may conclude that we shall be able to divine what is necessary to life by means of the internal sensibility. Have not the biological sciences demonstrated an analogous fact? The biometer applied to man has made it possible to reconstruct the absolutely average man, that is to say, the man whose body gives average measurements in every part; and these average measurements have been found, by means of the statistical and morphological studies of medicine, to correspond to "normality". Thus the average man would be a man so perfectly constructed that he has no morphological predisposition to disease of the organs. When the figure of a man was reconstructed in accordance with average biometrical proportions, it was found to correspond in a remarkable manner to the proportions of Greek statues. This fact helped to give a new interpretation to "aesthetic sentiment". It was evidently by means of aesthetic feeling that the eye of the Greek artist was able to extract the average measurement of every organ and construct a marvellous and exact whole therewith. The "enjoyment" of the artist was his enjoyment of the "beautiful"; but he felt even more profoundly that which contained the triumph of life, and distinguished it from the errors of nature, which predispose to illness. The triumph of creation can give an intimate pleasure to him who can "feel it"; errors, even slight, will then be perceived as discords. Aesthetic education is, in short, akin to the mathematical approximation towards the absolute average; the more it is possible to approach to the true measure in its extreme limits, and the closer we can get to this, the more possible does it become to have an absolute means of comparison for the consideration of deviations. The great artist is thus able to recognize the beautiful in a detail even in the midst of other discordant details; and the more capable he is of possessing an absolute sense of the beautiful, the more readily will he perceive any disproportion of form.

Something of the same sort may happen in the conscience in relation to the distinction between good and evil; the more so as the good stands for real utility in life far more directly than the beautiful, and the evil may be roughly said to represent danger. Have not animals, perhaps, an acute instinct of self-preservation, which dictates infinite details of conduct to them, both for the maintenance of life and for its protection? Dogs, horses and cats, and generally speaking, all domestic animals do not await the imminent earthquake quietly and unconsciously as does man, but become agitated. When the ice is about to crack, the Esquimaux dogs which draw the sleighs detach themselves one from the other, as if to avoid falling in; while man can only observe their amazing instinct with stupefaction. Man has not by nature these intense instincts; it is by means of intelligence and the sensibility of his conscience to good and evil that he constructs his defences and recognizes his perils. And if this intelligence of his, which is actually capable of transforming the world, raises him to such a supreme height above animals, to what a lofty eminence might he raise himself by developing his moral consciousness!

But on the contrary, man today is reduced to the point of asking himself seriously whether animals are not better than he. When man wishes to exalt himself, he says: "I am faithful as a dog, pure as a dove, strong as a lion".

Indeed, animals have always that instinct which is admirable, for it confers on them a mysterious power; but if man lacks sensibility of conscience he is inferior to the animals; nothing can then save him from excesses; he may rush upon his own ruin, upon havoc and destruction in a manner that might fill animals with stupefaction and terror; and if it were in their power they might set themselves to teach man, that he might become equal to themselves. Men without conscience are like animals without instinct of self-preservation; madmen rushing on to destruction.

What shall it profit man to discover by means of science the laws of physical self-preservation in its most minute details, if he has no care for that which corresponds in man to the "instinct" of his own salvation? If an individual has a perfect knowledge of hygienic feeding, of the manner in which to weigh himself in order to follow the course of his own health, of bathing and of massage, but should lose the instinct[1] of humanity and kill a fellow creature, or take his own life, what would be the use of all his care? And if he feels nothing more in his heart? If the void draws him to it, plunging him into melancholy, what does his well-nourished and well-washed body avail him?

Good is life; evil is death; the real distinction is as clear as the words.

Our moral conscience is, like our intelligence, capable of perfection, of elevation; this is one of the most fundamental of its differences from the instincts of animals.

The sensibility of the conscience may be perfected like the aesthetic sense, till it can recognize and at last enjoy "good" up to the very limits of the absolute, and also until it becomes sensitive to the very slightest deviations towards evil. He who feels thus is "saved"; he who feels less must be more vigilant and do his utmost to preserve and develop that mysterious and precious sensibility which guides us in distinguishing good from evil. It is one of the most important acts of life to examine our own consciences methodically,

---

[1] Montessori distinguishes throughout the impulses of man from the instincts of animals, although occasionally she also uses the word "istinto" (instinct) for the former (Ed.).

having as our source of illumination not only a knowledge of moral codes, but of love. It is only through love that this sensibility can be perfected. He whose sense has not been educated cannot judge himself. A doctor, for example, may be perfectly informed as to the symptoms of a disease, and may know exactly how cardiac sounds and the resistance of the pulse are affected in diseases of the heart; but if his ear cannot perceive the sounds, if his hand cannot appreciate the tactile sensations which give the pulse, of what use is his science to him? His power of understanding diseases is derived from his senses; and if this power is lacking, his knowledge in relation to the sick man is vanity. The same holds good of the diagnosis of our own conscience; if we are blind and deaf, innumerable symptoms will pass unobserved, and we shall not know on what to found our judgement. The tedium of futile undertakings will oppress us from the first moment.

On the other hand, it is "feeling" which spurs us on towards perfection.

1929 (3) Those who assert the absolute goodness of human nature have triumphantly claimed that this idea is the basis of our method, whereas those who maintain that mankind is completely corrupted by Original Sin have been among our harshest critics ...

In actual fact, it is not at all a question of absolutes in this instance. How ready we are to say that a child is doing something bad, when he does something to annoy us, or which alters our habits and disrupts our peace and comfort. Have we ever asked ourselves which of the actions a small child performs are good and which are bad? Have we never made the mistake of judging a child more by our own conventional standards than according to God's plan ...

The weakness and the possibility of transgression which persist in the child's soul, and in ours, as a consequence of Original Sin, ought in any case to be a reason for the most enlightened love on our part, for support combined with growing pleasure, and a noble Christian perfection of our attitude and actions as teachers. But this does not permit us, yet alone entitle us, to start to behave like stern judges, blindly handing out futile punishments. As a consequence of the same Sin, the child's body is also subject to pain and sickness, though this does not prevent his body from being the most perfect work of art which God has created, and which can develop the radiance of health, if we provide him with the correct nourishment and an environment free of disease ...

The fact that children in a Montessori school are better behaved, more obedient, more sociable etc., has nothing to do with the more fundamental question of actual good. A child who has enjoyed the spiritual care which our method offers (that is, apart from special religious education) has found an environment that is better suited to his development. *But this does not necessarily mean that the child is actually good from the perspective of supernatural virtue ...*

1949 (4) ... It is only much later when the time for "drawing the first sketch of man" is over, and the child, who has been more or less successful in realizing the design of life, begins to be *interested in outer things*, that envy at the success of others can arise. Things are different then and judgement with regard to "good and evil" can then be made. Then we may speak of defects of a moral order concerning society and the corrective intervention of education can be justified ...

... "An education of vastness" therefore is the platform whereon certain moral defects can be eliminated. The first step of education must be to "extend the world" in which the child of today languishes, and its fundamental technique consists in "freeing him from the shackles which impede his advancement". We must "multiply the motives of interest which satisfy the deepest tendencies buried in the soul. Invite him to conquer without limits, instead of repressing the desire to possess what belongs to those around him". On this plane, open to the realization of all possibilities, we can, and must, teach respect for the outer laws, established by that other natural power – the society of men.

In conclusion, the moral question, and hence that of moral goodness, cannot be discussed with regard to the "small child". Only when the child comes to the use of reason is it possible to bring the problems of philosophy into the field. Moral philosophers, however, deal with evil in much the same way by directing the individual to transcend its appeals with the aim of reaching God. In fact those who desire to fight against "Original Sin" do so by turning man towards the greatness of the Redemption.

1948 (5) ... Civilization has given man, by means of the machine, (1939) power much greater than his own. But for the work of civilization to develop, man must also develop. The malady from which our age suffers comes from the imbalance created by the difference in rhythm at which man and machine have evolved; the machine has advanced at an accelerated pace and man has remained behind. Man is dependent on the machine while it is he who must dominate it. Progress must not mean the triumph of materialism. It ought, on the contrary, "to elevate" man. Placing one's ideals at ever higher levels is exalting. We must teach the adolescents what our task on earth is. But the power man has gained from the use of the machine ought also to create new duties, an always higher morality.

Man by means of supranatural powers may perceive through glass infinitely small or distant things. He can make mathematical calculations that would have been completely inaccessible and even inconceivable to natural man. He can today listen to voices that have come a considerable distance. He can measure the waves that render communication possible. He travels at an always faster speed; he flies in the air and maintains himselves on the surface of the sea. The machine therefore confers on him an immense power, a power almost as fantastic as that of the heroes of fairy tales. The progress of the social surroundings is related to it. But if education does not help him to participate in such a world, he remains "outside society". Man with this "supernature" is the king of the earth, of visible and invisible things. He penetrates the secrets of life by giving birth to the flora and fauna that constitute such a supernature, causing products of the earth to progress by chemistry, transforming bodies as though by the help of a magic wand. This is the proof of the grandeur of collective humanity, to which each man can contribute. But it is also because of this that the man who has such power becomes dangerous. New individual and social morals are necessary in the new world – morals that give new directives on good and evil, on the heavy responsibilities individuals are assuming in regard to the whole of humanity, from the moment their power rises above that of their nature proper. The machine ought not to *replace the slave* in the new civilization …

… It would be good to follow this month's preparation period by a sort of examination, which would not relate to studies but to problems of conscience. It is, in effect, at this moment that the child makes a sort of debut into life. It is at this time that we must prepare him to fight against the evil forces which he will find himself. He must resist temptations. Also, we cannot let him present himself before the "prince of this earth" without any preparation: a résumé of what he has done up to now and an examination of conscience constitute a sort of admission to the entrance into life.

1949 (6) … When we gaze at the stars, twinkling in the sky, ever faithfully following their orbit, so steadfast in their position, do we think: "Oh! how good the stars are!" No, we only say: "The stars obey the laws that govern the universe", and we say, "How marvellous is the order of creation!"

A *form of order* in nature also appears in the behaviour of children.

Order does not necessarily mean goodness. This order does not at all prove that man "is born good" nor that he is born evil. It proves only that nature, in its process of constructing man, follows an established order.

Order is not goodness, but perhaps it is an indispensable way to attain it.

Also our outer social organization needs order as its foundation. The social laws regulating the conduct of citizens and the police force which controls them are of basic necessity in a social structure. Yet a government embodying these institutions can be bad, unjust and cruel. Even war, which is the least good and most inhuman feature of social life, is based on discipline and obedience on the part of the soldiers. The goodness of a government and the discipline it maintains are two distinct things. Similarly, in schools, there can be no education unless discipline is first obtained – yet there can be good and bad forms of education.

Here among these children, order came from mysterious, hidden, inner directives, which can manifest themselves only if the freedom permitting them to be heeded is given. In order to give this type of freedom, it was precisely necessary that nobody interfere to obstruct the constructive spontaneous activity of the children in an environment prepared so that their need for development can find satisfaction.

Before we can reach the point where we are "good" we must first enter into the "order of the laws of nature". Then from this level we can raise ourselves and ascend to a "supernature" where the co-operation of consciousness is necessary.

Regarding evil and badness, we must also distinguish "disorder" from a descent to a lower moral plane. To be disorderly regarding the natural laws which rule the normal development of the child, does not necessarily mean to be "bad". The English, in fact, use different terms to indicate the "badness" of children and that of adults. They call the former "naughtiness" and the latter "evil" or "badness".

We can now state with certainty that the naughtiness of young children represents a disorder regarding the natural laws of psychic life in course of construction. It is not badness but it does compromise the future normality of the psychic functioning of the individual.

1929   (7) *The dead dog:* A dead dog had been lying for several days in a sunny street in a town in Palestine. A group of men had gathered around the disgusting object. Some said, "Isn't it horrible!", others "Isn't it awful!", and they pushed it aside. A young man came along, stood looking at it for a moment, and then said, "What lovely little teeth it has!"

And, in fact, the dog's teeth were still white and shining. Then somebody asked, "Who is that young man, who can still find something beautiful about this dead body?" And the answer was – so the legend continues – "His name is Jesus, and he is the son of a carpenter from Nazareth".

This little story illustrates the existence of a sensibility that can see good wherever it might be found, and however slight or obscure it may be. Such a sensibility is a feature of that perfect love which is exemplified by our Lord Jesus Christ. And this love, which sheds its light on everything, is called "Caritas".

We must not confuse this type of love with vague forms of optimism. It does not make us perceive everything in the world as good, but only those things which are truly good and can thus be clearly distinguished from evil.

Our Lord did not see the dead dog as something beautiful, but he saw the one beautiful thing that had remained amidst the rest of the decaying animal. In the same way, the eye of a great artist immediately spots a truly valuable object, even when it is inconspicuous, and mixed in with many ugly or commonplace things. On the other hand, an uneducated man who is insensitive to beauty may perceive ugly things as pleasing, and be blind to the beauties of a real work of art.

The type of goodness which sees everything as good and for which evil does not exist is therefore something entirely different from the love that is required to become a good teacher of young people.

Sources: (1) *Mein Handbuch*, p. 113–119; (2) *The Advanced Montessori Method I*, p. 258–262; (3) *The Child in the Church*, p. 158–161; (4) *The Formation of Man*, p. 35–37; (5) *From Childhood to Adolescence*, p. 79–80; 83; (6) *The Formation of Man*, p. 32–33; (7) *The Child in the Church*, p. 62–63.

6. Education and Peace: "The Single Nation"

1932 (1) What is generally meant by the word *peace* is the cessation of war. But this negative concept is not an adequate description of genuine peace. Most important, if we observe the apparent aim of a war, peace understood in this sense represents, rather, the ultimate and permanent triumph of war. The primary motive of the wars of antiquity, in fact, was the conquest of land and the consequent subjugation of entire peoples.

Although man's environment is no longer the actual physical land but rather the social organization in and of itself, resting on economic structures, territorial conquest is still regarded as the real reason for which wars are waged, and throngs of men are still swept off their feet and troop to the colours under the influence of the suggestion of conquest.

Now, why do great numbers of men march off to face death when their homeland is threatened with the spectre of invasion? And why do not only men, but also women and even children, hasten to defend their country? Out of fear of what will go by the name of peace once the war is over.

Human history teaches us that *peace* means the forcible submission of the conquered to domination once the invader has consolidated his victory, the loss of everything the vanquished hold dear, and the end of their enjoyment of the fruits of their labour and their conquests. The vanquished are forced to make sacrifices, as if they are the only ones who are guilty and merit punishment, simply because they have been defeated. Meanwhile, the victors flaunt the rights they feel they have won over the defeated populace, who remain the victims of the disaster. Such conditions may mark the end of actual combat, but they certainly cannot be called peace. The real moral scourge stems in fact from this very set of circumstances.

If I may be allowed to make a comparison, war might be likened to the burning of a palace filled with works of art and precious treasures. When the palace is reduced to a heap of smouldering ashes and suffocating smoke, the physical disaster is complete; but the smouldering ashes, the smoke that prevents people from breathing, can be compared to peace as the world ordinarily understands it.

This is the same sort of peace that ensues after a man catches a disease, after a war is waged in his body between his vital energies and the invading micro-organisms, and after the man eventually loses the battle and dies. We very appropriately express the hope that the dead man will rest in peace. But what a difference between this sort of peace and the peace that goes by the name of good health!

The fact that we mistakenly call the permanent triumph of the aims of a war "peace" causes us to fail to recognize the way to salvation, the path that could lead us to true peace. And since the history of every people on earth is marked by one wave after another of such triumphs and such forms of injustice, as long as such a profound misunderstanding continues to exist, peace will definitely fail to fall within the range of human possibilities. I am not speaking only of the past, for even today the lives of peoples who are not at war represent an acceptance of the situation created between victor and vanquished. The former wreak merciless havoc, and the latter curse their fate like the devils and the damned in Dante's *Inferno*. Both are far from the divine influence of love; all of them are fallen creatures, for whom universal harmony has been shattered into a thousand pieces. And this chain of events continues to repeat itself, for all peoples have been alternately victors and vanquished and have wasted their energies in this terrible ebb and flow of their fortunes in the boundless tides of the centuries: "Watery deep to watery deep is calling".

We must bring the profound difference, the contrary moral aims of war and peace, into the clear light of day. Otherwise we shall wander about blindly, the victims of our delusions, and in our search for peace we shall come across nothing but bloody weapons and destitution. The prospect of true peace makes us turn our thoughts to the triumph of justice and love among men, to the building of a better world where harmony reigns. An orientation of our minds that clearly distinguishes between war and peace is only the starting point, however. In order to shed light on this subject, as on any other, a positive process of investigation is required. But where in the world is there a laboratory in which the human mind has endeavoured to discover some part of the truth, to

115

bring to light some positive factor with regard to the problem of peace?

Meetings inspired by the loftiest sentiments and the noblest wishes for peace have been held, it is true. But we shall never discover valid concepts on which to base a study allowing us to understand and unravel the causes of this awesome enigma unless we realize that we are faced with real moral chaos. There is no term but moral chaos to describe our spiritual situation, wherein a man who discovers a virulent microbe and the preventive serum that can save many human lives receives great praise, but wherein a man who discovers destructive techniques and directs all his intellectual powers toward the annihilation of entire peoples is praised even more highly. The concepts of the value of life and the moral principles involved in these two cases are so diametrically opposed that we must seriously consider the possibility that the collective personality of mankind is suffering from some mysterious form of schizophrenia.

Obviously there are chapters in human psychology that have yet to be written and forces that we have not yet mastered that presage enormous dangers for humanity.

Such unknown factors must become the object of scientific study. The very idea of research implies the existence of hidden or perhaps even unsuspected factors that are far removed from their ultimate effects. The causes of war cannot lie in well-known and thoroughly studied phenomena dealing with the social injustices suffered by workers in economic production, or the consequences of a war fought to the finish, because these social facts are too apparent and too easily recognizable in the light of even the most elementary logic for us to regard them as the deep-rooted or mysterious causes of war. They are rather the tip of the fuse, the last part to be ignited before the explosion that war represents.

1932 (2) ... In order to begin the task of reconstructing man's psyche, we must make the child our point of departure. We must recognize that he is more than just our progeny, more than just a creature who is our greatest responsibility. We must study him not as a dependent creature, but as an independent person who must be considered in terms of his own individual self. We must have faith in the child as a messiah, as a saviour capable of regenerating the human race and society. We must master ourselves and humble ourselves in order to be able to accept this notion, and then we must make our way toward the child, like the three kings, bearing powers and gifts, following the star of hope.

Rousseau sought to discover in the child man's pure and natural characteristics before they are side-tracked and spoiled by the influence of society. This is a challenging theoretical problem, and thanks to a fertile effort of imagination Rousseau was able to build an entire novel around it. Were a psychologist to deal with the subject in the abstract, he would doubtless view it in terms of an embryology of the human mind.

But when we for our part studied the newborn child, who turned out to have unsuspected and surprising psychic characteristics, we found something more than an embryonic mind. We were deeply moved at the discovery of a real and awesome conflict, a ceaseless war, that confronts the child from the very day he is born and is part of his life all during his formative years. This conflict is between the adult and the child, between the strong and the weak, and, we might add, between the blind and the clear-sighted.

The adult is truly blind to the child, and the child has real vision, a bright little flame of enlightenment that he brings us as a gift. Both the adult and the child are unaware of their own characteristic natures. They fight one another in a secret struggle that has gone on for countless generations and is becoming even more violent today in our complicated and nerve-racking culture. The adult defeats the child; and once the child reaches adulthood the characteristic signs of the peace that is only an aftermath of war – destruction on one hand and painful adjustment on the other – remain with him for the rest of his life.

The child for his part cannot lift up the fallen older man by lending him his own fresh strength and life-renewing vitality, because the adult becomes an adversary whose first gesture is to stifle him.

This situation is much more serious today than at any time in the past. By constructing an environment that is further and further removed from nature, and thus more and more unsuited to a child, the adult has increased his own powers and thereby tightened his hold over the child. No new moral sensibility has made its appearance to free the adult from the selfishness that blinds him, and no new understanding of the many changes in the human situation that are unfavourable to children has penetrated the minds of mature human beings. The age-old, superficial notion that the development of the individual is uniform and progressive remains unchanged, and the mistaken idea that the adult must mould the child in the pattern that society wishes still holds sway. This gross, time-hallowed misconception is the source of the primary conflict, even war, between human beings who by all rights should love and cherish one another – parents and children, teachers and pupils.

The key to this problem lies in the two different forms and goals of the human personality, one of which is characteristic of children and the other of adults. The child is not simply a miniature adult. He is first and foremost the possessor of a life of his own that has certain special characteristics and that has its own goal. The child's goal might be summed up in the word *incarnation*; the incarnation of human individuality must take place within him.

The child's work, aimed entirely at this incarnation, has vital characteristics and rhythms that are totally different from the adult's. That is why the latter is the great transformer of the environment and the social being *par excellence*.

If we think for a moment of the embryo, we may perhaps understand this concept more clearly. The one aim of the embryo within the womb is to attain the maturity of the newborn child. This constitutes the prenatal phase of man's life. The most vigorous newborn child will be the one who has developed in the womb in the very best conditions that a healthy mother can offer him, taking no special care other than to allow the new creature to live within her.

But man's later gestation is not as brief as the one in his mother's womb. The child goes through another kind of gestation in the outside world, incarnating a spirit whose seeds are latent and unconscious within him.

Delicate care is required to protect the child as he does his work, of which he becomes conscious little by little and which he performs by means of experiences in contact with the outside world. The child performs work with inner wisdom, guided by laws like those that guide every other task that is accomplished in the realm of nature, following rhythms of activity that do not have the slightest resemblance to those of the aggressive adult bent on conquest.

The concept of the work of incarnation or spiritual gestation as being completely different from the labours of the adult human active in the social order is not a new one. On the contrary, it has been solemnly and eloquently celebrated for many centuries and comes down to us with all the force of a sacred rite. There are two holidays in the year that all of us observe – Christmas and Easter. We celebrate them in our hearts and take time off from our social labours, and many of us attend religious services on these two occasions. What do these age-old holidays commemorate? One single Person. But the incarnation and the social mission of this Person are recognized separately and distinctly.

In the story of the life of Jesus, his incarnation lasts until puberty, until approximately the age of thirteen, when the young boy says to his elders, "How is it that ye sought me? Wist ye not that I must be about my Father's business?" This is a young boy speaking. He has not learned wisdom from adults, but rather, amazes and confounds them. Only later do we learn of the obscure life of the boy who obeyed his elders, who did his best to learn his father's trade, and who came in contact with the society of men in which he was to fulfil his mission.

Let us suppose now that the characteristics and goals of the independent life of childhood are not recognized and that

119

the adult takes those characteristics that are different from his own to be mistakes on the part of the child and hastens to correct them. At this point a battle will take place between the weaker and the stronger that is crucial for humanity, because the sickness or health of man's soul, his strength or weakness of character, the clear light or dark shadows of his mind depend on whether or not the child has a tranquil and perfect spiritual life.

And if in this delicate and precious period of life a sacrilegious form of enslavement of the child is practised, the seeds of life will become sterile, and it will no longer be possible for men to carry out the great works that life has summoned them to perform. Now the battle between adults and children takes place in the family and in the school, during the process that is still referred to by the time-hallowed word *education*.

When we took the personality of the child into account in and of itself and offered it full scope to develop in our schools – where we constructed an environment that answered the needs of his spiritual development – he revealed to us a personality entirely different from the one we had previously taken into consideration, with traits exactly the opposite of those attributed to him by others. With his passionate love of order and work, the child gave evidence of intellectual powers vastly superior to what they were presumed to be. It is obvious that in traditional systems of education the child instinctively resorts to dissembling in order to conceal his capabilities and conform to the expectations of the adults who suppress him.

The child bows to the cruel necessity of hiding himself, burying in his subconscious a life force that cries out to express itself and that is fatally frustrated. Bearing as he does this hidden burden, he, too, will eventually perpetuate mankind's many errors.

The question of the relationship of education to war and peace lies therein, rather than in the content of the culture passed on to the child. Whether or not the problem of war is discussed with children, whether or not the history of mankind is presented in this or that form to children in no way changes the fate of human society.

The failure, the weakling, the slave, and the arrested personality are, in short, always the products of an education that is a blind struggle between the strong and the weak.

The fact that the child has character traits quite different from those he was long believed to possess has been proved incontrovertibly after a quarter of a century of constant work,[1] not only in almost every nation that shares our Western heritage, but also among many other widely divergent ethnic groups: American Indians, Africans, Siamese, Javanese, Laplanders. After our initial experiences, there was enthusiastic talk of a method of education capable of producing astonishing results, but soon thereafter many people became aware of the reality and the importance of this phenomenon. One of the first books on the subject, entitled *New Children*,[2] was published in England.

We have a glimpse of a new kind of humanity, with the reassuring appearance of better men. Might it be possible to improve human nature? This might be achieved as follows: by replacing the deviations imposed during man's formative years by a normal process of development, and allowing man to attain psychic health.[3]

The man with a sound psyche is such a rare creature today that we almost never meet one, just as men with sound bodies were few and far between before the concept of personal hygiene helped mankind recognize the basis of physical health. In the moral domain man still finds pleasure in subtle poisons and covets privileges that conceal mortal perils for the spirit. What are often called virtue, duty and honour are no more than masks for capital vices that education passes on from generation to generation. The child's unsatisfied aspirations have an effect on him as an adult

---

[1] In 1907, Montessori officially opened her first Children's House in Rome (Ed.).

[2] Radice, Sheila, *The New Children*, London, 1920 (Ed.).

[3] This paragraph has been emended on the basis of archive manuscript Baarn, P 1, p. 17 ff. (Ed.).

and betray themselves in different expressions of arrested mental development, in moral defects, in countless psychic anomalies that cause the human personality to become weak and unstable.

The child who has never learned to work by himself, to set goals for his own acts, or to be the master of his own force of will is recognizable in the adult who lets others guide him and feels a constant need for the approval of others.

The schoolchild who is continually discouraged and repressed comes to lack confidence in himself. He suffers from a sense of panic that goes by the name of timidity, a lack of self-assurance that in the adult takes the form of frustration and submissiveness and the inability to resist what is morally wrong. The obedience forced upon a child at home and in school, an obedience that does not recognize the rights of reason and justice, prepares the adult to resign himself to anything and everything. The widespread practice in educational institutions of exposing a child who makes mistakes to public disapproval, and indeed to a sort of public pillorying, instils in him an uncontrollable and irrational terror of public opinion, however unfair and erroneous that opinion may be. And through these and many other kinds of conditioning that lead to a sense of inferiority, the way is opened to the spirit of unthinking respect, and indeed almost mindless idolatry, in the minds of paralysed adults towards public leaders, who come to represent surrogate teachers and fathers, figures upon whom the child was forced to look as perfect and infallible. And discipline thus becomes almost synonymous with slavery.

The child thus far has been deprived of the possibility of venturing on moral paths that his latent vital impulses might have sought anxiously in a world that is completely new to him. He has never been able to measure and test his own creative energies; he has never been able to establish the sort of inner order whose primary consequence is a confident and inviolable sense of discipline.

The child's attempts to learn what real justice is have been confused and misdirected. He has even been punished for charitably having tried to help schoolmates who were more oppressed and less quick-witted than he. If, on the other hand, he spied on and denounced others, he met with tolerance. The most rewarded and most encouraged virtue has been besting his classmates and coming out on top, triumphantly passing examinations at the end of every year of his life of perpetual, monotonous slavery. Men educated in this manner have not been prepared to seek truth and to make it an intimate part of their lives, nor to be charitable toward others and to cooperate with them to create a better life for all. On the contrary, the education they have received has prepared them for what can be considered only an interlude in real collective life – war. For the truth of the matter is that war is caused not by arms but by man.

If man were to grow up fully and with a sound psyche, developing a strong character and a clear mind, he would be unable to tolerate the existence of diametrically opposed moral principles within himself or to advocate simultaneously two sorts of justice, one that fosters life and one that destroys it. He would not simultaneously cultivate two moral powers in his heart, love and hatred. Nor would he erect two disciplines, one that marshals human energies to build, another that marshals them to destroy what has been built. A strong man cannot stand a split within his consciousness, much less act in two exactly opposite ways. Thus if human reality is different from what it actually appears to be in everyday life, it is because men allow themselves to be passive and are blown this way and that like dead leaves.

War today does not stem from hating an enemy. How can it, when today men fight against one nation one day and another the next, and tomorrow's ally is yesterday's enemy? The white man who boasts of being a highly civilized creature is no better morally than the merecenary armies of the past who would fight anybody, as long as they were paid. Nothing has changed, except perhaps the fact that today men destroy their own handiwork and treasures and suffer famine simply because they have been ordered to do so. The Egyptians were wise enough to make a distinction between the work of building their civilization and the waging of war. They therefore paid Phoenician troops to fight their battles while their own people cultivated the land and engaged in public works projects. But we "civilized" nations confuse the two things.

Faced with the difficult social problems that cause such grave concern in our time, better men than we are would use their intelligence and their forefathers' hard-won victories in the battle to become civilized to find solutions other than war. Otherwise why should man be possessed of intelligence? And what point is there in our possessing the riches accumulated for us by the wisdom of our forefathers? For a better man, war would not even be a problem; it would simply be a barbarous practice diametrically opposed to civilized life, an absurdity completely beyond the comprehension of the new man. Modern warfare is actually a scourge which signifies only outward punishment for moral failings that obscure the human mind. The solemn and inspired voice of Jonah was sufficient to vanquish war, when he cried, "Turn back and repent, or Nineveh will be destroyed!".[4] It is up to man to choose his fate, and the day that his weapons fall from his hand will mark the beginning of a radiant future for mankind.

1936 (3) Men with the best minds on earth gather today in answer to a call to solve life's most urgent problems.

Peace is a goal that can be attained only through common accord, and the means to achieve this unity for peace are twofold: first, an immediate effort to resolve conflicts without recourse to violence – in other words, to prevent war – and second, a long-term effort to establish a lasting peace among men. Preventing conflicts is the work of politics; establishing peace is the work of education. We must convince the world of the need for a universal, collective effort to build the foundation for peace.

---

[4] This sentence has been supplied from archive manuscript Baarn, P 1, p. 20 ff. (Ed.).

KEYS TO THE WORLD

Constructive education for peace must not be limited to the teaching in schools. It is a task that calls for the efforts of all mankind. It must aim to reform humanity so as to permit the inner development of human personality and to develop a more conscious vision of the mission of mankind and the present conditions of social life. These aims must be achieved not only because man is almost totally unaware of his own nature, but also because for the most part he does not understand the workings of the social mechanisms on which his interests and his immediate salvation depend.

The most characteristic phenomenon of modern life is the sudden change in our social conditions. The outward change is obvious, for scientific discoveries and their practical applications have brought about amazing changes in our physical environment. But this change is perhaps not so apparent at deeper and more essential levels underlying these outward changes in our civilization. This second level on which change has occurred is proof nonetheless that thanks to economic mechanisms and communications, men have in fact managed to become united in their material interests.

This achievement indicates that new goals have emerged in the field of these interests themselves, and it is necessary that men be consciously educated to fulfil them, for if men continue to regard themselves as national groups with divergent interests, they will run the risk of destroying one another. This is the crux of all the questions regarding peace.

As a consequence of these changes, war is now pointless and cannot yield any material profit. The [first world] war in Europe has already shown that the victors have not gained new energies and benefits from their victory, as victors did in the past. An entirely new phenomenon has occurred: defeated peoples have become a danger, a burden, an obstacle. The victors must aid them and help them get back on their feet. A conquered nation today is an illness that all of mankind suffers. The impoverishment of one nation does not make another nation richer; rather, all nations decline. Destroying one nation is tantamount to cutting off one hand in the mistaken hope that the other hand will thereby become twice as strong.

125

We are all a single organism, one nation. By becoming a single nation we have finally realized the unconscious spiritual and religious aspiration of the human soul, and this we can proclaim to every corner of the earth. "Humanity as an organism" has been born; the superconstruction that has absorbed all man's efforts from the beginning of his history has now been completed. We are living this reality. We have proof of it in the almost miraculous powers that today are enabling man to rise above his natural condition. Man now flies higher and more confidently through the heavens than the eagle; he has mastered the invisible secrets of the energy of the universe; he can look up into the skies and the infinite; his voice can cross the world's seas, and he can hear the echoes of all the world's music; he now possesses the secret powers of transforming matter. In a word, contemporary man has citizenship in the great nation of humanity.

It is absurd to believe that such a man, endowed with powers superior to those of nature, should be a Dutchman or a Frenchman or an Englishman or an Italian. He is the new citizen of the new world – a citizen of the universe.

This being the case, it is no longer possible to assume the existence of nations with divergent interests. Separate nations with their own borders, their own customs, their own exclusive rights no longer have any reason for being. There will always be human groups and human families with different traditions and languages, but these cannot be sufficient reason for the existence of nations in the traditional sense of the word: they must unite as constituent elements of a single organism or die. The great bell calling men to rally around the one banner of humanity is a summons on which our very life depends. Today all men are in touch with one another; ideas circulate through the air by radio from one end of the earth to the other, recognizing no national boundaries; groups sharing the same ideas are being formed all over the world, and men can no longer cling to the medieval mentality of the Palleschi and Piagnoni in Italy.[5]

---

[5] These were the two parties for and against the Medici family in Florence.

KEYS TO THE WORLD

Modern agitators are, however, attempting to take over these enormous powers that henceforth must belong to humanity as a whole.

There are only two paths before us: we must either prove worthy of our great achievements or die as a result of them. It is absurd to fight each other for material well-being or national defence or the triumph of one social system or another.

Our era is a time of adjustment to material conditions that have undergone vast changes. We have conquered our physical environment and overcome our purely natural limitations. We have mastered invisible powers and taken the place of the Jupiter Tonans of the Greeks and the gods of the Hellenic peoples. But we are not yet fully aware that we have done so, and this is precisely what prevents us from becoming brothers in order that this superworld may become the Kingdom of Heaven.

Man must be educated to realize his greatness and to become worthy of the powers that are his. If, in the Rome of the Empire, the Roman citizen needed to be aware of his dignity, it is even more necessary that today's citizen of the Universal Empire become aware of his.

The human personality has remained as it was in the conditions of the past: man's character and mentality have remained unchanged, and he does not understand the destiny and responsibility that he now has because of the new powers at his disposal. Man, in short, has not kept pace with the progress that has been made in his external environment; he remains timid and confused, fearful and susceptible to blind submission to authority, to a return to paganism or even barbarism, because he feels overwhelmed by the superworld in which he lives.

Modern psychologists have spoken of the dangers that threaten the individual who is a victim of a so-called inferiority complex; but what can we say of the perils that threaten all humanity because man, the king of the universe, trembles with fear and is so overcome with depression that he is tempted to do away with himself?

127

BASIC IDEAS OF MONTESSORI'S EDUCATIONAL THEORY

Our principal concern must be to educate humanity – the human beings of all nations – in order to guide it toward seeking common goals. We must turn back and make the child our principal concern. The efforts of science must be concentrated on him, because he is the source of and the key to the riddles of humanity. The child is richly endowed with powers, sensitivities, and constructive instincts that as yet have neither been recognized nor put to use. In order to develop, he needs much broader opportunities than he has been offered thus far. Might not this goal be reached by changing the entire structure of education? Society must fully recognize the social rights of the child and prepare for him and the adolescent a world capable of ensuring their spiritual development.

In order to do this, all nations would have to reach an understanding, to bring about a sort of truce that would permit each of them to devote itself to the cultivation of its own human members in order to find therein the practical solutions to social problems that today seem insuperable.

Perhaps the attainment of peace would then be easy and close at hand, like waking from a dream, like freeing our-selves from a hypnotic spell.

Sources: (1) *Education and Peace*, p. 6–9; (2) *Ibid.*, p. 14–21; (3) *Ibid.*, p. 24–27.

7. Man and the World: "Cosmic Education"

1946 (1) To give an idea of what we mean by Cosmic Education it is necessary to touch upon the background of the question, i.e., the cosmic theory. This recognizes in all creation a unifying plan upon which depend not only the different forms of living beings, but also the evolution of the earth itself. This idea, although it includes the foundation of evolution theory, differs upon the causes and the finality of the progressive changes of the species. The progress of life through its struggles and its defences is not due to change. Life progresses according to a cosmic plan and the purpose of life is not to achieve

128

perfection along an unlimited line of progress but to exercise influence and to achieve a definite aim upon the environment. Geology has long shown the close relation between life and earth and has considered the life which cloaks the whole surface of the earth as the "biosphere" necessary to the building up of the earth ...

It was recently proved on observing the functions of the animals that their behaviour, their individual mode of acting in the environment has the purpose not only of maintaining themselves, but above all, of carrying a specific item in the complex task of the upkeep of the earth and of maintaining harmony on it. To realize this one need only think of the first brilliant example given by Darwin concerning the close collaboration between flowering plants and insects. The insect which goes to seek nourishment in the flower of the plant carries out unconsciously an altruistic task, the pollination of the flowers. He ensures in this way the crossing and the survival of the plants. Similarly all other animals by the process of feeding themselves or seeking food carry out a "cosmic" task which contributes to keep nature in a harmonious state of purity. Each kind works for the whole and upon the work of each depends the possibility of the life of the whole. These cosmic tasks have been wisely distributed among all the behaviour which urges it irresistibly to some task which is useful for the community. Ecology is a new science which studies these correlations. When one observes the generality of this contribution one cannot but wonder about Man. Is Humanity the only parasite who lives among useless struggles and immense work merely to keep itself living? Is it possible that only Man spends his brief span of life suffering in this terrestrial world to no purpose? This cannot be so. It is evident that the cosmic theory must include also man among the agents of creation. We must observe this behaviour in order to find out what are his essential functions which contribute to the upkeep and the development of the earth. It immediately springs to the eye that man exerts a "modifying function" upon nature. From the beginning of time he worked (and he continues at first

129

sight to do so) for his own benefit, but living upon the earth he leaves a trace of his existence and enchanted path. Wherever man passed the flowers became more beautiful, the plants richer, the jungles became forests and the waters were distributed ...

And man himself, in building that which we call civilization, multiplied his powers to the point that he overcame all the limitations of nature and rose above the conditions that were his at the moment of his first appearance upon the earth. He to whom nature has given only two feet to walk upon, can today cross the earth by mechanical means which transport him from one end to the other, passing through continents as well as oceans and even through the wide spaces of the atmosphere. Human intelligence has become almost all-powerful and today has arrived at a point where it can dominate the energies of the world and penetrate the most intimate secrets of life ...

And finally, in the present epoch, the union of all humanity seems to have been reached unconsciously, for today man exchanges not only the produce of his material activity but also the thoughts, the discoveries, and all the products that arise from the work of pure intelligence. One thing is very clear today: that humanity is effectively united. Yet this union was not a conscious task, a conscious aim. On the contrary, men have remained so unconscious of the fact that the evidence of the union has been realized more under the form of the threat of destruction than under the guise of a superb triumph of creation.

One thing still evades the intelligence of humanity and that is the consciousness of their terrestrial destiny and of the fact that the whole of humanity is so intimately united that it forms but one organized energy. The revolutionary movements of our days are a sign of the great crisis from which "the Universal Consciousness" of humanity is about to be born.

From the extreme dangers of our days the vision is born of the necessity that men should with their conscious will and with their sentiment, seek to find the "adaptation" to present conditions, thus forming one universal harmonious society. This is the aspiration to which today humanity clings, urged by the supreme appeal of seeking its own salvation. But how to attain this if not through a "direct preparation" of the new generation, i.e., through education? …

Men did not take care of humanity. Its growth was neglected and left to chance and thus remained inferior in development to the development of the environment in which he lives. He is without orientation and without control over his own creation.

… it is through a childhood modified and freed from the ties of unconsciousness, of weakness, of psychic deviations and of ignorance, that it is possible to act by giving a new form of intellectual culture and by cultivating new sentiments for humanity. It is this later part, culture, that which represents the study to be carried out in the schools, the universal syllabus that can unite the mind and the consciousness of all men in one harmony, that we intend by "Cosmic Education".

This education must take its departure and spread from one centre, the cosmic plan of creation. In this concern, all that has developed during the different civilizations achieved by different groups is a preparation for the great and supreme triumph of the human agent who has already reached dominion over all things and who must now find dominion over himself. It has prepared a united and all-powerful energy in a union which, though unconscious, is real and which consists of all human individuals in one organized body.

In the universal syllabus of studies to which the new generations must apply themselves, all the items of culture must be connected as different aspects of the knowledge of the world and the cosmos. Astronomy, geography, geology, biology, physics, chemistry are but details of one whole. It is their relation to one another that urges interest from a centre towards its ramifications. There is besides this the other part which concerns the directing of the consciousness towards humanity. The cosmic construction of human society must be the core of the study of history and sociology …

BASIC IDEAS OF MONTESSORI'S EDUCATIONAL THEORY

An ardent admiration towards this prodigious humanity must be the fundamental sentiment of the new generations. They must feel the pride and privilege of belonging to humanity. Man must appear as a sacred being of creation and as the greatest marvel of nature and the sentiment of "gratitude and love" for all the advantages that we enjoy in life must be aroused with every step that is taken in the field of culture. No object must be made use of without the thought that some unknown man produced it. The morsel of bread, the handful of rice, the dress, the house, the road, the means of transportation, everything was given to us by men. Their effort and their sacrifice for us must always be present in our consciousness …

To offend humanity is to be blindly and barbarously ignorant. From this education must arise the persuasion that mutual help among men is the most direct form of universal defence. The need or the inferiority of a people are a real danger for the whole of humanity and it is in the interests of all to find the means to satisfy those needs and to uplift men from their state of inferiority. This has been understood in the physical field, where the unhygienic condition of any one spot is a danger also for the people who enjoy perfect hygiene conditions and it has been found that the best way of assuring one's own health is to better those conditions. Human society must reach a level of average welfare where the necessities of life can be satisfied for all people.

This concept resembles that of some religions. Without doubt, the cosmic concept has an affinity with the "Unity of God the Creator", recognized in many religions. Unity among men as well as help for the weak form part of the Christian spirit and of that of other religions. These two concepts answer to every lofty religious institution. But that which stands out in the cosmic theory is not only the utility of giving help to man, but the justice which must be rendered to humanity for its merits and the recognition of the fact that we owe all to its efforts. In religions, by contrast, everything which is good and which we enjoy, is attributed to the mercy of God. In social life, however, much of what we enjoy must be laid to the credit of the work of man. We might repeat here "Give unto God that which is God's and unto Man that which is Man's". It is necessary to arouse that religious sentiment of gratitude that was given to God also towards man. Religious respect for sacred humanity as the effective dispenser of God's mercy must be aroused in the coming generations. An offence to human life must be felt as a sacrilege. If this is not so, the "Curse of God" will visit us again and again in the shape of disastrous wars for having disregarded man, the sacred provider of the common wellbeing of us all.

1935 (2) In simple words – if God moves beings intelligently, to man He gives intelligence itself. If there is a divine communication between all created beings here there is a more direct one. (Human instinct can communicate with the divine. It is as if man alone understood that he must take this line).

Sources: (1) *The Child, Society and the World*, p. 106–113; (2) *Ibid.*, p. 98.

C. Practical Texts

1. The Children's House

1977 (1) *Helene Helming, Our Children's House*

Before us stretches the long, light grey two-storey building, with the blue-painted door in the middle which gives on to the little hallway between the Children's House and the classroom. These belong together, and are united in one house. We were able to achieve a smooth combination of the Children's House and the school into a uniform area for the children to live in. The not overlarge, close-set windows at the front and back have frames which are painted blue outside and red inside, and are a pretty sight when opened in summer. The house is surrounded by the garden, adjacent to which is a playground. Sunflowers bloom in the front garden during summer, climbing up to the low-set windows which the children can open themselves. Opposite, there is a building belonging to a gardener, with many fruit-trees. The hut is built behind houses along a street, on a plot of land next to an area of allotments. Thus the noise from the street does not reach the house, and nature is close at hand. In the winter, boards and coconut shells with food for the birds are hung outside the windows, and the sunflower seed is collected for this purpose. The flowerbeds outside the house are a blaze of colour in summer, and the children pick and cut flowers from them for their rooms, or to make bouquets for special occasions. Through the window, the teacher can see children working in the garden, clearing the paths, removing dead leaves or caterpillars.

We pass through the small gate in the wooden garden fence, across the garden and up the two steps to the front door, and on into the entrance hall, where the coloured hangers for the children's coats hang on a polished rail. Above the rail there is a shelf for caps and hats, and on the floor there are racks for their shoes. Adjoining the hall are toilets and washing facilities, which individual children can easily reach from their rooms.

On the left, we enter the room for the three to six year olds. It is before 9 o'clock, and not all the children are yet present. From 8 o'clock onwards they trickle in and begin "to work", after the assistant has met them in the hall and helped them remove their hats and coats and change their shoes. They enter, say hello to the teacher, and go to a piece of work they have chosen themselves. They do not all begin together. The way the children begin to work depends on what they feel like doing in the morning, and this is best satisfied if they immediately start to do something on their own or to work freely in groups of twos or threes. A sense of community develops later over breakfast. But first each child fetches the material he desires and sits down at a spot he has chosen himself. The room is bright throughout with the light from its many windows. In the Children's House, we have arranged most of the tables in an oval pattern, with each table at some distance from the other. In one corner of the room stands another, larger, round table with several small chairs, and near the windows there are a few tables scattered around, each with a chair.

On arrival, one child will only make up his mind about where he wants to start after some hesitation, and will do various things, until he finds his main piece of work. Another child will aim straight for a particular activity. He may have the "work" from the previous day already in mind. Many a child will continue a piece of work, e.g. a drawing, that he has started the day before and put away in a drawer. On shelves along the partition opposite the door, and on separate tables, all the individual objects lie ready and waiting. The children easily find their way to what they need, or are prompted to try something new. With occasional exceptions, there is only one of each item, a fact that highlights its importance and enhances its appeal. It also helps to ensure that the children's work remains diverse and maintains a balance, without the teacher's intervention. If an item of material is already taken, then the other child must wait until it becomes available.

At 9 o'clock, all the children are present. It has been agreed with their mothers to keep to this routine. Thus, especially during the first part of the morning, most of the children can be seen engaged in various types of individual work. One child is working with the solid insets, another is drawing with the aid of the geometric figures, another has the colour charts in front of him, two older children are shading the third box of the colour chart to make a popular game, of the sort that the children in a Children's House have devised themselves. One child has fetched a rug from the corner where they are kept rolled up and tied with a ribbon, spread it out on the floor and brought the purple rods, which he now lays out on the rug, and to which he adds the numbers one to ten. At one window, a girl is sitting and painting with watercolours, at another, one is sitting with a

135

weaving frame; beside her is a box with coloured scraps of wool, from which she selects the threads that she draws with a long needle across the taut warp. The children like weaving. There are several weaving frames of the sturdy type that sit firmly on top of the desk, which we ordered from the carpenter, and especially in the pre-Christmas period the children like to weave something, from which the teacher helps them to make bags and other things for their mothers. On one desk, a child has spread out an oilcloth. He fetches the vases with flowers from the other tables, together with a bucket and a jug with some water, and he pours the water from the vases into the bucket, then pours fresh water from the jug into the vases, which he refills with the flowers, after removing the dead parts. He replaces the vases with the newly arranged flowers, empties the remaining water down the sink in the next room, fetches a cloth and wipes the oilcloth dry, and, if necessary, he wipes up any water he has spilt with the floorcloth. This keeps him busy and absorbed for a long time, and if he doesn't spill any water, he has done well. Beside the door to the next room there is a small wash-stand, without running water, but with a bowl, a jug, and a bucket, a soap dish, a nail cleaner and a nail brush. In this environment, a child is engrossed in doing something he likes. He will wash his hands, less because he needs to than because he takes pleasure in carefully pouring water from the jug into the basin and, after using it, into the bucket, and in performing all the individual acts associated with washing one's hands. During a "lesson" together, the teacher showed the children how to wash their hands by slowly performing the action for them. – An older child has gone into the garden and cut some flowers. Now he goes over to some shelves, on one of which there are a number of different vases. With the help of the teacher, he selects one of them for his flowers and arranges them on the table. On a table by the window there is an aquarium. As they pass by, the children like to stop for a while in front of it and watch the fish or the tadpoles that change so strikingly.

KEYS TO THE WORLD

On the wall of the room, opposite the door, hangs a coloured picture of the Virgin Mary, the Holy Mother with the divine Child, with a wall vase on one side, and a sconce with a candle on the other. A few children come, one lights the candles, another starts to sing a song, a small group joins in, then one of them blows the candle out again. This spot with the picture is also suitable for children who have not prayed at home to say their morning prayers. This they do quite naturally and as a matter of course, after the teacher has suggested it during a talk together, and occasionally given a lead.

There are also children sitting at the round tables, with picture books in front of them. Two are enjoying the popular book "The Thick Greasy Pancake", while a third child has an animal picture book, one of the well-known "Blue Books". There are only a few picture books on the shelf on the wall, but they are changed from time to time.

Around 10 o'clock (the time is not fixed precisely, so that the work is not suddenly interrupted), a child gets up and starts to lay the long table in the next room. The children gradually fetch their sandwiches from their bags, and one after another they sit down to breakfast.[*] A few children pour out some milk, and they all start to chat away happily. After breakfast, the children wash up at the low sink, and put the dishes away in a cupboard. They carefully fold the coloured tablecloths and handle the fragile china with care. The children then continue their activities in the large room, if the pace of work demands, or they do exercises together, there are stories or singing, and at the end of the week there is a discussion about whether everything in the Children's House has been fine, or whether changes are needed in the future. The teacher has the opportunity to draw attention to various things, even to the fact that it is Sunday or a holiday.

---

[*] Breakfast is taken in various ways in the Montessori Children's Houses. If space is restricted, each child takes what he needs for breakfast to his small table, and in his own time. If there is a round table, a type of group develops there, with different children taking part.

137

BASIC IDEAS OF MONTESSORI'S EDUCATIONAL THEORY

Not many children are there in the afternoon. It is good if the parents can keep most of them at home, since the Children's House is no substitute for the parental home with its benefits and educational potential, but complements the domestic environment. When the weather is good, the teacher spends a lot of time outside during the afternoon with those children who do come. She does gardening with them, they build things in the sandpit, take out the balls hanging in a net beside the door, or go for walks in the nearby park.

Such activity, which was not the same every day, but was varied and enriched by different incidents, took place in our "hut". This was not a new building, but had been brought here from elsewhere, given a fresh coat of paint, and adapted. It would not be hard to imagine a more suitable building, but children do not need a luxurious environment the value of which is measured in financial terms, and a certain roughness and primitiveness is even beneficial to them, if this does not involve anything inappropriate. But without scope to play, and suitable, well-organized material made ready for their senses, hands and minds, they do not thrive. As we have seen, the inclusion of movement is a fundamental principle of Montessori's educational theory. The child incarnates his spirit through everything he does, the spirit relates the movement to itself and in the right environment becomes aware of the possibilities of both physical and spiritual movement. Children become nervous when living in close confinement with adults, their movements are erratic and their spirit becomes restless if the process of incarnation and self-formation cannot take place. Under present circumstances, it is vital to prepare for them a natural but structured environment in the Children's House and school in which they can be fashioned through purposeful play.

This prepared environment is a whole, which is shaped by the life of the child. Its characteristic feature is its pervasive order, which is however not purely of practical value. Associated with order is the beauty and richness of life. On entering a Children's House and seeing something of the life the children lead, it is obvious how happy they are. The children's joy convinces us that by preparing and fostering such an environment we have united with the benevolent powers of the child's divinely created nature.

2. The Montessori School

1980 (2) *Hans Elsner: Everyone has the right to be himself**

The view at the moment is that having fewer children in a class is by itself a big step on the road to individual education. The idea is that the teacher, having more time, can devote greater effort to the individual child. While some of the class work on their own, he can sit down beside the "slow" pupil and give him individual help to catch up.

Who would not take advantage of this opportunity in his class? I think all teachers are just waiting for the chance. But the question arises as to whether individual education is really a veiled form of remedial teaching or even a form of private tuition sanctioned or planned by the State. Of course, learning is here on an "individual basis", but the real concern is why it should be so.

If we declare by law that all children of the same year are ready, willing and able to attend school all at once and on the same day, then this date will also coincide with the start of remedial teaching in schools. It is obvious that other solutions must be possible. There will always be "slow" pupils, just as there will always be "quick" ones. At Maiglöckchen, this surprises nobody. Father B. has two daughters. They attend the Montessori Children's House opposite the school. Bärbel is of school age, and now goes to the school and not to the Children's House. Elsbeth is a year younger, and still has to go to the Children's House. This is what the law says, but Elsbeth suddenly takes a different view of the matter, and

---

* The following lines are a report based on practical experience. Above all they should afford the reader a glimpse into the real life of a Montessori primary school. References to the ample primary and secondary literature on Montessori's educational theory are contained in the bibliography.

refuses to continue to attend the Children's House without her sister. Her behaviour is very obstinate, stubborn and quite unreasonable, as we adults say. She cries a lot and eats very little – her idea of a strike.

Then her father visits me, seeking advice. "Couldn't we keep Bärbel away from school for another year, and then send both of them to school next year?"

I said to him, "We'll do it the other way round. Buy Elsbeth a satchel and send her along tomorrow!" By law, she was three months too young, but she knew better, as the outcome showed. This was Elsbeth's first day at school. She happily took her place beside Bärbel – four weeks later than her "big sister". She already knew some of the children. At first they must have stared in surprise, but that was all. Elsbeth was at school.

In a Montessori primary school class, several years always work together. Elsbeth met children there from the 3rd. and 2nd. year, and from the new 1st. year. She already partly knew those from the 1st. year, and now there was also a child of "pre-school age". A class with this range of ages must work and learn differently from the single-year classes normal in all schools.

At the heart of the Montessori Method is the child's voluntary work, which features right from the start of school in the morning. The children go to their classes as soon as they arrive at school, and are immediately able to begin a piece of work that they have chosen themselves. Each child starts individually. Voluntary work in the Montessori sense means that the pupil decides on his own and of his own free will to do something, to begin a piece of work. Of course, he can also decide not do anything for the moment. He may wish to wait or speak with others, he may be undecided or just waiting for someone, so as not to be alone.

There are sufficient reasons why a child should not rush headlong into a piece of work on entering the classroom. But actually there are even more reasons why he should do so.

I think that it is just as important for the child, on his arrival in school, to find the classroom ready for learning at school as it is for him to find the room to make a free decision about work.

Occasionally, some children are already in class an hour before teaching officially begins. They don't always come so early because they are no longer able to bear being away from school, but often enough that is precisely the reason. An individual start is as much a part of the Montessori school as the first unconscious breath is part of each new day.

Sooner or later, all the children have arrived and found what we call work. The official start of classes is only observed by a glance at the clock.

There are many reasons why children arrive earlier at school in the morning. The most important ones are that they want to learn, and that they like working. In addition, their friends are there, as well as the teacher and many interesting things – the "material". Everything combines to make the school a nice place. Nevertheless, were it not for the wish, and indeed the necessity, to learn on their part, they would not arrive before eight o'clock.

Bernd's mother brings her son as far as the school steps. She actually wanted to accompany him to his seat – he has just recovered from a broken arm. On seeing me, she immediately reveals her astonishment at Bernd's enthusiasm: "Last night he was simply crazy about getting to school really early today. He kept talking the whole time about his 'horse work' which he has to get on with. As far as we could tell, he is painting something to do with horses, and writing as well. And this morning his first thought was his 'horse work'".

Andrea, a 3rd-year pupil, came really early to school for several days because she wanted to do arithmetic with the multiplication table. She didn't want anyone to get there before her, and claim the material for themselves. She gets up extra early so that she can do her important work. She is popular in the class because she is so friendly, but now she thinks only about her work.

Apart from Kai (4th year), all the children are busy. I ask him, "Don't you want to continue the history chain you were

141

doing yesterday?" He answers, "I am still waiting for Marco. We work together". Kai wants to wait, and not finish the work they had started on his own. It is not the case here that he is reliant on Marco in the sense of lacking independence. In the reverse situation, Marco might have given me the same answer. One thing emerges clearly from Kai's statement in this instance. Children think differently about work and its results than we adults do.

The individual decision to work together with another child has created a kind of unity in decision-making. Kai resolves to start a new piece of work rather than to destroy this unity. Individual learning is anything but individualistic learning.

For us adults, this is a surprising insight, which is subsequently confirmed by Marco himself. When he returns to school after five days off sick, both resume work at the very same point where they had previously stopped.

I cannot easily explain this kind of behaviour with words like perseverance, concentration, determination or consistency. I think that what we are seeing here is joy at *working together*.

We all know that children copy what we adults show them. Maria Montessori requires meticulous lessons in the use of her material, which as a rule are given to the individual child, so that he receives the help he needs to do things on his own. The lesson is meant to be like a hand which helps him "to reach the fruit" more easily.

The lesson given by the teacher, which introduces the child to the material and its use, is absolutely essential, with the material being something like a key that unlocks a door.

For voluntary work, the classroom must be properly prepared, if children are to be free to choose what they want to do. The material provided must fulfil quite specific requirements. The children's readiness, their ability and their inner wishes place demands upon the way the class is organized. The *prepared environment*, as Montessori calls it, embodies

Illus. 1: A classroom in the Montessori primary school, Cologne.

both freedom and guidance. The Montessori material has its own proper place. It is stored away properly on shelves and in cupboards. The children not only accept this strict order, but they expect everybody else to observe it as well. Practical considerations are important here. In our class there is an agreement: Put everything back in *the place you wish to find it next time*.

Why would the children not observe this agreement?. It is after all what *they* want for *their* class. It is not the teacher's doing. He offers them assistance so that the order works – order intended as a precondition for successful learning.

It has been my experience that as a rule younger children tend to carry outer order to excess rather than to neglect it. I have never been able to detect any pleasure in disorder. And why? Well, who would break off the tip of his pencil when he is just about to write a story?

A side room is of course an integral part of the class, and naturally new objects are also often available for the environment. Both the teacher and the children bring along things from their lives in the afternoon or on Sunday which they want to show to the others. This may be a piece of wood from the garden, a new book, a letter from grandfather, 24 chewed hazelnuts, stones, flowers or a few fragments and bones from the pit next door. Even at home our children live in a "rich" environment, and I think that our school must have the space and the time to accommodate these things as well. Children show an interest in their world, and they have a need to understand this world. The interest gives rise to expectation, the need to demands.

When the school was being painted, some material had to be packed up and stored away. For instance, the "animal and vegetable trees" (an item of material for showing order in the animal and vegetable kingdoms) were unavailable for a fortnight. Peter (a 2nd year pupil) had to interrupt his work on the "animal tree". Well, what can be done in a case like this other than to change the subject? It is good for children to find out through such circumstances that there are reasons why their own wishes must be put to one side.

KEYS TO THE WORLD

In the school, this is accepted as a matter of course. From Peter's mother, I learned that, after waiting three days, the boy had complained angrily about the workmen, who to his way of thinking were too slow. He and his brother thought about how he might gain access to the material that was packed away. To give his protest the necessary edge of seriousness, he said, "I must carry on. I'm afraid I shall forget everything again!" Yes, many will say, with *such* children you really can do voluntary work! But, I would object, there are no *such* children. There are only our children, and they are like everyone in the world – each is different.

So that they may indeed be different, we have different years in the groups. Six year old children sit beside ten year olds. And why? Each works according to his needs. One child is still unable to read, another is already writing long stories. But they not only sit side by side, they soon get to know one another quite well. And this happens in the most natural way possible. They talk, they work, they have breakfast, they laugh, they quarrel, they help one another and learn together. They also get in one another's way. But it makes a difference whether all these things only take place among children of the same age, or between older and younger ones. Help given by a pupil of the same age always smacks a little of judgement, especially when school marks make this inevitable.

For mixed years, helping one another comes naturally. A little girl will ask an older one, "Will you fetch the buzzard for me from the cupboard?", "Where are the scales?", "What is the name of this letter?", "I can't do up this button". Helping becomes something natural. But the younger ones help the older ones as well. This is not part of a set plan, it's just the way things are. All the children have had experience of voluntary work from previous years. The older ones were also young once. From this perspective, the primary school offers the chance to study social virtues for four years.

It is not because the teacher wants it to be like this, but, as I have said, it is just the way things are. And because it is like this, I also say that these are really virtues, and not educational objectives.

145

BASIC IDEAS OF MONTESSORI'S EDUCATIONAL THEORY

This may sound to many like "schoolboy Latin", and they will think, "but actually, we have outgrown that kind of thing". Individual work in the school draws its life from the group. Just as small fishing boats on the high seas always stay close to the parent ship, so that they can meet up with the other boats at any time, so it is also with individual work in Montessori classes. But each child is also trained to break away from the group at the right moment, for ultimately children must learn to stand on their own two feet.

Whenever one of our former pupils who now attend other schools turns up again, he comes to visit his old school-friends, the classroom and the teacher in equal measure. They not infrequently come during the voluntary work period. "It's all right for you, you can finish your work!", or "But all our work is marked by the teacher!" They still feel part of the group, although the new class is a new path that they were ready to follow right from the start.

We agree on a more substantial task.* As only eight children are taking part, the afternoon will have to do. The eight are from the 3rd and and 4th years. We drive out of town to the area where the Romans had their estates, remains of which we want to find. At home we have been studying the map. We want to see what is lying on the surface of the field and has been washed clean by the rain. We may find some fragments of material, perhaps the remains of some roofing tiles. I take a handful of pieces that were found earlier from the bag, and show them to the children. I stick them halfway into the earth, so that they can all see what the pieces look like in the field. Each child has a bag in his hand and gumboots on his feet. We are prepared.

I knew that we would strike lucky. The field has been ploughed up, but is not yet under cultivation. The earth has been loosened by the rain, and fragments are protruding everywhere. In no time, the children become "hunters and gatherers (of fragments)". We all know what happens in such

---

* The following example shoud be viewed in the context of Montessori's ideas about a "Cosmic Education"; cf. chap, B. 7 of this volume (Ed.).

Illus. 2: Children gather fragments on a site previously inhabited by Romans.

Illus. 3: The finds are washed …

situations. They bend down and search, pick something up, look at it, examine it, ask questions, size it up, and perhaps throw it away or put it straight into the bag. I think that researchers also work like this. On the way home, I feel a sense of satisfaction, something you always experience after a good haul. Part of the main task is finished.

Now the finds are washed. It is as if the fragments are being discovered anew. Without the dirt, they appear different. It goes without saying that we handle them carefully, laying them out on newspapers, so that they can dry overnight. What can be done with such fragments? Similar questions, such as "are they valuable?", or "what would it cost to buy them?", have already been asked and answered yesterday. We want to arrange the finds, but first we agree on how to interpret them.

The fragments come from vessels. There are pieces from the bottom of a vessel or from the rim. Bits of handles are

Illus. 4: ... then arranged, marked and labelled.

easy to recognize, as are pieces from the neck of a vessel. The part between the rim, neck and bottom we simply call the "belly". The majority of our finds consist of fragments of roofing tiles.

After the "units" have been sorted, we arrange all the pieces in rows according to size. One schooldesk is not enough to hold our collection. Now the marking and labelling takes place. All at once, everyone realizes: through our efforts to establish order, the Roman period has suddenly emerged from the scattered heap of fragments in the field, and is now very close to us. The children have held history in their hands.

We now discuss the craftsmanship, material and culture involved. It is really grand to be so intimately acquainted with the past.

Arranging the pieces helps both the children and me to understand. We have isolated one difficulty after another, as Montessori says, and in the end we know that this is an experience that we have all shared.

Two of the children in this group carry on working. It is hard for them to accept that it might not be possible to reconstruct a whole jug from the numerous fragments. What finally emerges from all this, however, is the subject of Roman pots and jars. The children start to read, to draw and to paint.

More frequently, children at the Montessori school come to a topic (or a technique) the other way round. Guido is practising drawing circles with the compasses. At the next table, Esther starts to work out areas. Two friends have written a long sentence on a strip of paper, and set about parsing it. Karen has decided to fetch the box with the objects in it and to match the name-cards to the objects on her own. As far as their subject matter is concerned, all types of work can have a contagious effect. It is like throwing a stone into the water – the circles spread outwards. The children start to form teams.

Only *one* pupil can sit and write at the dictating machine. He selects his own dictation. Its speed and length and the number of repetitions are up to him. Indeed, he can place the check-list alongside, and if necessary can just look at it. The range of dictations is large, and he can begin with really easy ones. "What do you do", one visitor asked, "if a pupil writes 20 dictations in succession, and thus uses up time for other subjects? It could even go on for days!" Well, it could go on for weeks. I would probably just take note of it, but that's all. I have never known children write 20 dictations in succession – but they have the opportunity to do so. Would we for instance read a book several times without good reason?

Thus, major pieces of work in biology, mathematics or geography can last for weeks. If children can persevere and finish their work, we also share in their satisfaction.

Voluntary work is not the only aspect of a Montessori school. Subject and classroom teaching are just as important, and depending on circumstances provide either a supplement, a starting-point, an overview, or a context.

But individual learning offers children a special opportunity for self-development and self-discovery. By making his own decisions, a child forms an attachment to a thing. In work he learns his own abilities and limitations. He becomes aware of his personality and learns to accept it. Everybody has a right to be different. Marks do not make the man, nor does a curriculum.

Maria Montessori has shown us a method of education which she developed solely by observing the behaviour of children. I believe that those who follow this method will no longer feel the need to pursue all those pedagogical ideas which invade schools from time to time, are revived, and then disappear. These ideas are not geared to the individual needs of children, and assume that man is not by design orientated towards independence and community. They believe they must first create the qualities that go to make up man.

A educational theory based on constructs leaves behind an insipid taste wherever its language is used.

Let us create the space and the opportunity in our schools for our children to retain their independence, and to continue to develop it. And we should give the things that have already been buried the time they need to come quietly to light!

3. The Montessori Grammar School

1948 (3) *Maria Montessori, her ideas for a secondary school*

(1939)

During the difficult period of adolescence it is desirable to have the child live outside his habitual surroundings, outside the family, in the country, in a peaceful place, in the bosom of nature. There, an existence in the open air, individual treatment, a sound diet ought to be the first conditions for the organization of a centre of studies and of work.

This theory is based on the formula that has already been widely tested throughout the world. The creation of secondary schools far from the large cities, in the country or in small cities, goes back a long time. Such institutions have prospered in large number in England for the use of all classes of society, even the most privileged (Eton, Harrow, et cetera), and the same principle may be found in the universities of Oxford, of Cambridge, et cetera. These schools enjoyed such success in England and the United States that cities have been built up around the formerly isolated universities. This is the case of a large part of the modern universities of America.

Life in the open air, in the sun, a diet rich in vitamins furnished by the nearby fields are the auxiliaries so precious to the body of the adolescent; while the calm environment, the silence, the marvels of nature satisfy the mind and are conducive to its functions of reflexion and meditation. In addition, the rhythm of daily life at college can better harmonize with the demands of study and work, while family life must rather conform to the demands of the life of the parents.

Our plan, though, is not a simple replica of the universities in the country or in small cities, because it is not the rural environment itself to which such value is attached, but rather to rural work and to "work" in general, together with the social sense conferred by production and earnings.

The observation of nature is not only an enrichment of the mind from the philosophical and scientific points of view. It is also at the base of a number of social experiences that engender the study of civilization and human life.

It is not intended to turn the students into peasants by means of "rural work". The intensive methods of modern argriculture were not achieved by the manual work of man alone but equally by his invention. It is thanks to science – a product of civilization – that man has created a sort of "superconstruction".

Therefore, the work of the soil is at the same time an introduction to nature and to civilization. The work of the soil is the approach to limitless scientific and historical studies. As for the harvest that ensues, it constitutes an initiation to the fundamental social mechanism of production and exchange, the economic base on which society rests.

This form of work, then, introduces the children to the heart of social life by experience and study.

If we have called this organization *Erdkinder*, "The Children of the Soil" or "Rural Children", it is because we are, in fact, dealing with children who are penetrating civilization from its origins – that is to say, from the stage where peoples, settling on parcels of land, commenced a peaceful era of life and of civil progress. The nomads, in the meantime, remained barbarians and warriors.

The children's school or, more exactly, their house in the country or in the small city must provide the opportunity for social experience for them because there their lives are lived on a larger scale and with greater possibility of freedom than with their families.

Various forms of activity should adjoin this establishment. Halfhearted efforts would lead to failure. Work in the hotel, the store, and the farm will complete the whole.

A modern farm requiring a number of scientific and manual labours presents the chance to produce, then to exchange, and also to enter into direct contact with society through the store or sales stand.

KEYS TO THE WORLD

By providing a hotel annex, "The Rural Children's Hotel", the school affords itself the opportunity of initiating the children into all that such an enterprise entails.

Such a house, receiving both boys and girls, should be directed by a married couple who, in addition to the material functions, exercise a moral and protective influence on the youths. It would be a family house.

By participating in the administration of the house, the young people acquire experience in all the various branches offered by the hotel enterprise, from the search for comfort to the social and material organization to the surveillance and control of the finances.

Since the small children have proved to us that they were able to keep the house clean and orderly, to serve at table, to wash plates, or to be responsible for the dishes, it will be easy for adolescents to run a hotel. It is a profession for whose preparation special schools have been established.

The hotel with its multiple activities could extend beyond the scope of "residence-hotel" of the children themselves. It could, while remaining simple and rustic, be designed to receive short visits of the families of the pupils, thus permitting them to acquaint themselves with the way of life of their children in school, and contributing to the economic equilibrium of the institution.

The hotel, conceived in a modern design of artistic simplicity and brightened by children free of artificial restraints, ought to furnish a whole range of activities capable of developing the sense of the artistic in one's dwelling.

Finally, another social institution offering very important experiences is the "store". It will be the social centre.

A store or sales stand established in the nearby city permits the *Erdkinder* to bring and sell there the products of the fields and gardens together with other products of their labour, and, should the occasion arise, the products of others' labour. They would thus be able to dispose of the products of poor neighbours or tradesmen which do not pass through the normal channels of commerce.

153

This enterprise should always have its particular characteristics and conserve the tradition of the past when personal talent was expressed in the fabrication of each object.

The store could be considered as the historic resurrection of a medieval shop, which used to be a meeting place and, one could even say, a symbol of sociability. It also offered an artistic aspect. It was consecrated and dedicated by means of a ceremony to some religious idea. It was used for selling and buying in honest simplicity. It constituted a sort of public institution for small commerce where individual exchange of objects took place, bringing with it the exchange of news and sentiments. It was part of the social life.

The ancient custom of mixing business with friendship and the establishment of personal contacts is reminiscent of the past. This custom has every chance of being revived among the joyful, enthusiastic youth avid for variety.

The store, in addition, makes necessary a carefully planned initiation to exchange and commerce. It must teach the art of satisfying a request, of exchanging words and ideas with the man in the street, as well as the strictly accurate keeping of books.

1959 (4) *H.-J. Jordan, What is a Montessori secondary school?*

I have already indicated that there are other differences in day-to-day teaching in the various "Montessori secondary schools". For the moment, I wish to confine myself to describing what they have in common. Later on, I shall deal with the school in Utrecht as typifying their form of organization.

The pupils are divided into "groups". We use this expression rather than the term "classes", in order to avoid any confusion. In a Montessori school, therefore, a "group" means a team of pupils working together, who for at least a year share the same workroom. Such a workroom has some features in common with the small and homely Montessori classrooms we are familiar with from the primary schools. There are no forms, but chairs and tables, or even desks, which the pupils (in certain cases upon instruction from the "teacher") can position as they wish, or as seems appropriate for team-work.

The composition of these groups varies in the different schools. Sometimes they comprise pupils of about the same level of development, another time they will include pupils from two or more years, or even members of the separate sections (e.g. classics, modern languages, mathematics etc.). The first type is easier to organize, but runs the risk of creating a class in the old sense of the term which will advance at a common speed, so that some pupils will again fall behind with their work and will have to be removed at a certain stage. The other, mixed form is more like what we see in Montessori primary schools, something which Dr. Montessori also regards as an essential benefit to team-work and social training, since each individual pupil is either the youngest or the oldest in the group. The younger pupils are encouraged by what they see the older ones doing. The older pupils are able to help the younger ones, which as a form of non-compulsory revision is also very useful to them.

In answer to the objection that the more homogeneous group is really a class in disguise, it can be argued that the completely organic structure of the school allows a great deal of flexibility and individual thought in decision-making, which goes at least some way towards dispelling the serious reservations that exist about pupils staying-down. It is not actually necessary for pupils who fall behind in some subjects in one of these "groups" to repeat everything, including the subjects they have mastered. That will discourage them, and costs valuable time.

The room where such a group works may be thought of as being something like a university department or the reading room of a university library, where the students sit for much of the day, either alone or together, and work on one subject or another. Supervision is by a teacher or a "group director", whose function I shall outline elsewhere. In a group like this there is normally a happy and peaceful atmosphere or working environment, of the kind we are familiar with in Montessori preparatory schools and primary schools. The

155

pupils are able to talk quietly, circulate freely etc. The group director merely has to make sure that there is not too much noise, as this disrupts the work.

If there is sufficient room, such a "group" can be quite large, larger even than the already high maximum in our normal classes. If the "group" is properly organized, there is no reason why any problems should arise.

While the group director helps to ensure the necessary quiet and outer order, he very carefully observes the development of each individual pupil, gives help and advice where necessary, or even gives active assistance, as far as he is able. Besides the group director, who is mostly an influential figure from the field of education with a particular interest in the particular educational situation, there are the teachers for the various subjects. In most schools, there are varying numbers of subject rooms and rooms for practical work which are used for teaching, or where the subject teachers help, test etc. smaller groups or even individual pupils. Whoever enters the room of such a "group" will find most of the pupils there individually occupied with the subject of their choice. The room may however be half empty, because some of the pupils are attending a lesson or because others have a compulsory period, perhaps with the mathematics teacher, or are doing practical work in biology, natural history or chemistry.

There are thus regular subject classes, free work and help periods (in which the pupils help one another or can call on the assistance of the teacher), as well as compulsory work periods for certain subjects. The way this is arranged differs in the individual "Montessori secondary schools".

A brief description of the organization of teaching and of the school

There would be little point here in my describing the various ways in which Montessori secondary schools try to implement Maria Montessori's methods on the basis of one approach or another to the organization of the school and of teaching. This is something I have already broadly described, and if I now go into detail, I am choosing to describe the organization as it exists in my own institution. That way I shall be certain not to make any mistakes. Moreover, in my school, particular attention has been paid to allowing the pupils' individual potential for development to be realized. The conventional group structure of the class has been avoided as far as possible. But, please, do not draw the erroneous conclusion that I consider our attempted solution to be the only correct one. In practice, however, it does fulfil the relevant expectations in many areas.

The composition of the groups of pupils at the Utrecht Montessori secondary school is, with the exception of the first and last groups, much more heterogeneous than in other Montessori establishments. The first group comprises only pupils newly arrived from primary school, the last group only those who hope to be able to sit their final exams in a year. Even in the first group there is very wide variation with respect to the pupils' progress (level of achievement). In the composition of the groups in between, four at present, areas other than just level of achievement are taken into account, though the latter is not ignored. Factors which carry at least as much weight in deciding the groups are: age, intellectual maturity, the wish or disinclination to work with certain other pupils, and a preference for one or other of the group directors.

In order to give the pupils a clear idea of the subject matter – and to be able to assess their progress properly – this is divided up into so-called "tasks", which are given numbers. Sometimes the pupil must accomplish these tasks in the given order, and sometimes their order is not fixed. A task comprises too much material on its own and is often further subdivided, whereby even within one task the order can be selected. These tasks relate primarily to the subject matter, which the pupils can assimilate by working on their own with the aid of special textbooks, simple schoolbooks or written assignments. For instance, in the teaching of Dutch a task may comprise some exercises in stylistic composition, grammatical exercises, insertion exercises, learning a poem by heart, doing a construction, and preparing a project. The

157

project must be presented to a group of pupils, and certain periods for this are included in the timetable. A pupil who has prepared a project (or in higher groups for instance a discussion of a book), reports to the subject teacher and is then told when the project may be presented. When the various subparts of a task have been completed, something for which the help of the group director, the subject teacher or an older pupil may be requested in certain cases, mastery of the material must be demonstrated.

How this is done is up to the subject teacher. It may involve examining the material the pupil has learned, something which is mostly done in private, and is thus in many respects a benefit. Or a test-card is completed, where, e.g., in mathematics, the pupil must show thorough assimilation and acquisition of the material, by means of oral tests or something similar. If the subject teacher is convinced that the task has been adequately mastered, this is recorded in the task book, which every pupil possesses, and which is like a book for preliminary examinations.

If the task has not been adequately mastered, then the pupil is required to make various corrections. Different grades (such as very good, good etc.) are not given. A tick against the task always indicates that it has been adequately completed. Only in special cases, for instance when, in spite of much effort and work, the result is still unsatisfactory, is the task marked with an asterisk. Ultimately, a pupil can pass through the school even with an "unsatisfactory" mark in one or two subjects. (Cf. in Germany the possibility averaging out marks under the regulations governing promotion).

The demands which our Montessori secondary schools make on their pupils are actually greater than in the majority of "classical" schools. It is simply not possible to achieve satisfactory results through brief and superficial revision or a lucky break in an oral test

As far as the recording of standards is concerned, there are also the so-called "course-tasks". These are given to pupils who have regularly attended a particular course and have achieved satisfactory results. The completed tasks are variously recorded on special cards by the group director, the pupils themselves or the headmaster. This way it is possible to provide a practical summary at any time, for use by the parents or at a meeting.

In theory, this method would make it possible for a pupil to choose one subject every time and to complete all the associated tasks right up to the last year before the final examination. While we consider it right in principle to allow the pupil a certain amount of variation, free choice of subject and choice of subject combinations, the variation should not become too extensive. In order to encourage equal appreciation of all subjects and also to provide some performance indicators which make the pupils feel that they have "made an important step forward", we employ a system of grading corresponding to procedures used in the workplace (that of Jonkheer Kees Boeke). The new pupils of the so-called A-group are called "novices". Their colour is green. Once they have learned the subject matter, i.e. a certain number of tasks, corresponding to approximately three years in a six-year secondary school, they are promoted by a decision of the committee to "pioneers". The pioneers, the "fiery Voortrekkers", whose colour is red, can be promoted to "candidates" (white) after two years, if they have completed the necessary tasks, *and* if the teachers' committee assumes it will be possible to prepare them for the final examination in the course of a year. The last and highest group of pupils must however again be homogeneous and is given a great deal of collective tuition, because it must ultimately be prepared to reach the same goal simultaneously. Since the pupils have by then achieved a high measure of independence and are spurred on by the imminent prospect of finishing, the difficulties of a more "classical" method of working are no longer so keenly felt, the more so since the pupils are already treated more or less as students.

Of course, the division "by years" that I use is theoretical. Depending on a pupil's natural abilities and capacity for work, success will come sooner or later. But it is an advantage of our method that a pupil who for some reason has got behind (through problems in adolescence, illness etc.) always has the chance to catch up. This opportunity is quite frequently utilized.

The courses are divided into optional and compulsory categories. These are quite clearly indicated, and the novice knows exactly which courses he must have attended in order to achieve promotion. The choice of the year in which he wishes to attend the relevant course is also left to him in certain cases. These courses have more in common with small-scale lecture courses than with ordinary school lessons. There is no need for oral testing or corrections, as these are better done another time. The number of course periods can therefore be limited, and their content can be more focused. They can serve to encourage individual work or provide a summary for pupils who have completed certain tasks on their own, or briefly treat a related subject. It is best if the courses do not last for a whole year, so that pupils have the chance to join, should they happen to complete their own work a little later, or something like that.

Needless to say, the choice and preparation of a work schedule is not left entirely in the hands of the pupils, but they receive advice from the subject teachers and group directors about which courses they should attend. The question of whether it is detrimental to leave a certain subject aside for a while depends on the importance attached to that subject. But in particular cases, care is taken to see that the subject is continued in each case, for example by attendance at a course, even at a time when the pupil is not working on his own in the subject. The attraction of this method of working – notwithstanding the considerable difficulties it inevitably involves – is its great flexibility, which allows us to adapt everything to the requirements of the individual pupil.

The way the day is organized, there are first a number of course periods between 8.30 and 11. These are limited to half an hour each, which in most subjects seems to be sufficient time for a focused "period" that will hold the pupils' attention.

In other cases, a *"double period"* is built into the time-table, that is, two lots of thirty minutes together.

After a short break comes the so-called optional period, in which the pupils can either work quietly in the room of their group, or seek advice from a subject teacher, correct their work or do oral tests. There are no courses during this time, so that (for an hour and a half a day) it may also be devoted to practical work.

The afternoon resumes with three course periods (of 30 minutes each). There then follows the so-called eighth period, which the pupils can use for "extracurricular activities" like acting, music, table tennis, chess and whatever else they want to do. Whoever so wishes, can of course also continue with his own work.

One of these "eighth periods" is set aside each week for a reading, a lecture on art, a concert, a film, a school council, a so-called forum (a voluntary gathering of pupils with shared interests). An important aim of this is to find speakers who will tell the pupils something from and about their their own occupation, in order to inform them about the various opportunities in economic life and society. Attendance at these events is optional.

The "eighth period" every Friday – the last schoolday of the week – is reserved for the great "school assembly" or "school congregation".

In our school, many things are arranged by the pupils themselves. Thus group discussions are held under the supervision of the group representatives. In this way, we aim to include the pupils in the organization of the school. Since our regime seeks to avoid high-handedness where possible and we almost never use the conventional forms of punishment, we need to find other ways to continue to appeal to the consciences of the pupils and to their sense of responsibility. For this reason, we also start the week with a collective gathering. This promotes the cooperation and cohesion of the pupils and the groups. Team spirit also asserts itself when the groups try their strength against one another or even against the teachers by playing sport during the main lunch-break. In this way, we aim above all to embody the social element in the organization of our school.

Besides the simple time-table, which shows which courses are taking place, and their times, we also have the "place table", which shows the time and the place where particular subject teachers can be found each day, and where they hold their meetings. Since course periods certainly do not take place during all course times, teachers are also available in between times, while not all pupils have teaching in every course period. In such cases they just continue to work on their own in the rooms for their group.

Sources: (1) from Helming, Helene, *Montessori-Pädagogik*, Freiburg 1977, p. 29–33; (2) from Elsner, Hans. Jeder hat das Recht, er selbst zu sein, in: Lichtenstein-Rother, Ilse, *jedem Kind seine Chance*, Freiburg 1980, p. 14–28; (3) from Montessori, Maria, *From Childhood to Adolescence*, p. 105–109; (4) from Jordan, H.-J., Was ist ein Montessori-Lyzeum? in: *Mitteilungen der Deutschen Montessori-Gesellschaft*, No. 1/1959, No. 1/1960.

4. A Sequel: Montessori in the Area of Special Education

1989 (1) *Karl Neise, Montessori and Remedial Education*

As an assistant doctor in the paediatric section of the psychiatric hospital of the University of Rome, Maria Montessori first came into contact with so-called "idiot" children in the late 19th century. When she observed that one such child was able to use his hands in a purposeful and creative way, she became convinced that these children constituted an "*educational* rather than a predominantly medical problem" (Montessori, 1969, p. 26).

While seeking suitable methods and materials for the education of the feeble-minded, she came across the work of the French pioneers in this area, Itard and Séguin. After sitting in on the lectures of Edouard Séguin's successor Bourneville, in Paris, around 1900 she introduced teachers in Rome to the education of the feeble-minded. Together with colleagues at a public institution, the "Scuola magistrale ortofrenica", she developed educational methods for treating feeble-minded children. For more than two years she was director of the State School for the Feeble-Minded in Rome. This all-day school was attended by pupils who had been removed from primary schools as hopeless cases. Subsequently, an Institute of Medical Education was added, in which not only these children, but also children from the lunatic asylum in Rome were given educational support.

During these two years, Maria Montessori, together with medical colleagues, herself trained the teachers in Rome who were to carry out educational work at the Institute. From her they learned about the observation and education of the mentally handicapped. Montessori gave a class herself, and worked as a supervisor for her colleagues from 8 o'clock in the morning to 7 o'clock in the evening. "Those two years of practical work provided me with my first real claim to be an educationalist" (Montessori, 1969, p. 27).

Her first experience in the field of education was thus acquired working with handicapped children (loc cit., p. 25 ff.). She believed from the start that the methods she had employed there could also be used with normal children, but she was first able to prove that even such severely mentally handicapped individuals could be given specific help. She remained firmly convinced by this intuitive vision of the potential for the development of children at special schools.

Montessori's education of the handicapped was based on the methods used by educationalists working with the feeble-minded at the time of the French Revolution and during the following century. The doctor and teacher of the deaf and dumb, Jean-Gaspard Itard, became one of the first French pioneers of education for the feeble-minded through his scientific description of the eight years he spent trying to educate the "Wild Boy of Aveyron", who had grown up in the wild away from any contact with humans. Itard's attempts at education were founded on the careful observation and systematic sensory training of the "Wild Boy" on the basis of sensualism.

Séguin refined the methods of his predecessor in ten years of work in Paris, and was the first to develop systematic sensory material for the education of the feeble-minded. In 1846 he published his findings (Séguin 1846). After a further 20 years of experimental work with handicapped schoolchildren in the United States, he published an expanded edition of his book there (Séguin 1866). In this second edition, there was a shift of emphasis. He now spoke of the "physiological method", with which he wished to treat and cure idiocy. This gave the method an importance of its own, more strongly orientated towards medicine, and as such it gained greater autonomy.

In addition to the time she spent attending lectures in Paris, Montessori visited England and Germany, to acquaint herself with methods suitable for educating the feeble-minded. Basing herself on Itard and Séguin, she systematically developed their approaches, especially in the areas of sensory and physical training, but also in the teaching of reading, writing and arithmetic. We can understand the great public response to her first educational successes if we bear in mind that Montessori achieved something which at the time was considered impossible: children from the "asylum for idiots" had passed a state primary school examination after two years full-time attendance at Montessori's first special school. They were able to read, write and do arithmetic: "I succeeded in teaching some mentally retarded children from the lunatic asylum to read and to do neat and exact handwriting. These children were subsequently able to sit and even to pass an examination in a state school together with normal children". (Montessori, loc cit., p. 32).

At the time, people talked of "miracles", and wanted to learn more about the method that was able to bring about such astonishing phenomena in the field of education, though Montessori suspected that the notion of a "miracle" would disappear if "normal" children were also given the opportunity to develop in an environment better suited to their educational needs than that found in conventional schools. She recognized the fundamental difference between the mental capacities of feeble-minded and normal children.

KEYS TO THE WORLD

As early as 1866, Séguin had pointed out in the expanded American edition of his book on the "physiological method" for the treatment of "idiots" that his method, which was based on the individual physiological and psychological study of each pupil and the subsequent translation of these studies into individual programmes of education, could likewise be applied to the education of normal children. He even hoped that this would lead to a complete regeneration of mankind.

Montessori thought she could hear the voice of "someone crying out in the wilderness" in these comments by Séguin (loc cit., p. 35), and she began her pioneering work with normal children, after studying philosophy, educational theory and psychology at the University of Rome. On January 6, 1907, she opened her first "Children's House" in a public authority building in the poor quarter of San Lorenzo in Rome. Here she was able to test and develop the practical knowledge and methods she had acquired with handicapped children on normal intelligent three to six year old children from a socio-economically deprived background. In mentally handicapped seven to twelve year olds, there are certain similarities to the intellectual achievements of normal three to six year olds.

Montessori believed that the method which enabled a mentally retarded individual to make such considerable mental and spiritual progress ought likewise to promote the healthy development of the physical and mental powers of non-handicapped children. She hoped that her educational work with three to six year olds would be able to prevent many later social anomalies or language problems in normal intelligent children (early diagnosis, prophylaxis!).

In the course of this work with normal nursery school children in San Lorenzo, Montessori experienced what she was to call in her own lifetime "the discovery of the child". She observed previously unnoticed phenomena of child behaviour, especially the "polarization of attention", the deep meditative concentration of children and its "normalizing" effect. These new discoveries led to the development of

BASIC IDEAS OF MONTESSORI'S EDUCATIONAL THEORY

Montessori's educational theory for non-handicapped children. From then on, Montessori herself did no further work in the field of special education.

In principle, the "prepared environment" for normal children developed since the San Lorenzo period also provides an ideal system for promoting the education and teaching of handicapped children and young people. In the case of auditory or visual defects, for example, the sensory material provides valuable help with compensatory or differentiating stimulations by allowing the isolation of difficulties and through its unlimited potential for repetition. Thus deficiencies in the sensori-motor sphere are evened out or offset, e.g. in the deaf or blind. Corresponding exercises for developing the accuracy, differentiation and speed of processes of perception in the tactile, kinaesthetic, olfactory, gustatory, auditory and visual spheres stimulate the cognitive development of the handicapped in a manner suited to the individual. There is also simultaneous training in motor activity, since the sensory materials teach accuracy of movement. In the same way, Montessori's "exercises of daily life" lead the handicapped child towards ever greater independence and self-reliance. Montessori's didactic material as "materialized abstractions" follows the principle of "from simple to complex".

The mixed-age classes that Montessori had deliberately set up since the San Lorenzo period accomodate the wide range of differing levels of development in the handicapped, and allow and encourage the pupils to learn from one another by imitation and social communication. The interactions that Montessori wished to encourage between pupils at different levels of development indirectly stimulate linguistic communication among the handicapped pupils.

The absence of sanctions and competitive situations also enables handicapped pupils to develop intrinsic motivation and automatic learning processes that lead to more realistic levels of self-esteem. In an environment prepared with the needs of (special) education in mind, even a handicapped child can find the pace of development that is appropriate for him, and is thus able to enjoy fulfilment and happiness in his life.

I myself have seen how in Montessori schools for the mentally handicapped (all with recorded intelligence quotients below 55), these pupils worked with concentration for more than two hours on activities they had chosen themselves using Montessori materials. They conveyed an impression of happiness and contentment.

In the debate about the integrative education and instruction of handicapped and non-handicapped pupils, Montessori's educational theory is meanwhile gaining more and more recognition as the best possible option. For twenty years, work on integration, as for example in the "Sunshine Project" (*Aktion Sonnenschein*) in Munich, has been progressing on the basis of Montessori's theory (Hellbrügge, 1988/89). This model has prompted the formation and foundation of numerous new integrative educational institutions. In Borken in Westphalia, a new privately sponsored model enjoying state recognition and strongly geared towards Montessori's basic ideas has been thriving for many years (Integrated Montessori Education in Borken, 1984). Here, integration can be encouraged from infancy right up to secondary school level, and a genuine attempt is also being made to implement Montessori's theoretical proposals for the instruction and education of 12 to 18 year olds.

Besides practical reports on the application of Montessori's theory to the education of the handicapped, there are several empirical scientific studies on this subject which demonstrate the superiority of Montessori's theory over conventional methods of teaching the mentally and educationally handicapped (cf. esp. Argy [1965], Kohlberg [1972], Neise/ Suffenplan [1984]).

Literature: Argy, W.P.: Montessori versus Orthodox. In. *Rehabilitation Literature*, vol. 26, 10, 1965, 294–304; – Hellbrügge, Th. (ed.): *20 Jahre Aktion Sonnenschein und Kinderzentrum München. Jahresbericht 1988.* Munich 1988/89; – *Integrative Montessori-Schule Münsterland e.V.: Gemeinsam leben lernen, Konzept und Erfahrungen.* Borken 1984; –

BASIC IDEAS OF MONTESSORI'S EDUCATIONAL THEORY

Kohlberg, Lawrence: The development of children's orientation toward a moral order. In: *Vita humana*. 1963, 3, 11–33; – Kohlberg, Lawrence: Montessori für kulturell Benachteiligte. In: Hess, Robert/Meyer-Bear, Roberta (ed.): *Frühkindliche Erziehung*. Weinheim/Basel 1972, 111–126; – Montessori, Maria: *The Advanced Montessori-Method, vol. II*. Madras 1965; – Id.: *Die Entdeckung des Kindes*. Freiburg 1969/⁸1987; – Neise, Karl: Das lernbehinderte Kind und die Montessori-Pädagogik. In: Hellbrügge, Th. and Montessori, M. (eds.): *Die Montessori-Pädagogik und das behinderte Kind*. Munich 1978, 156–180; – Id.: Möglichkeiten und Grenzen der Montessori-Pädagogik bei Geistigbehinderten. In: Hofmann, Th. (ed.): *Beiträge zur Geistigbehindertenpädagogik*. Rheinstetten 1979, 98–108; – Id.: Empirische Untersuchungen über Effekte Montessori-orientierten Unterrichts bei geistigbehinderten Schülern. *Z. f. Heilpädagogik*, 1984, 6, 389–397; – Séguin, Edouard: *Traitement Moral, Hygiène et Education des Idiots*. Paris 1846; – Id.: *Idiocy and its Treatment by the Physiological Method*. New York 1866; – Suffenplan, Wilhelm: Empirische Untersuchungen über Effekte Montessori-orientierten Unterrichts bei lernbehinderten Schülern. *Z. f. Heilpädagogik*, 1984, 6, 398–413.

1989 (2) *Theodor Hellbrügge, The discovery of the relevance of Montessori's educational theory to handicapped children*

It seems remarkable that a method of medical pedagogy like that of Maria Montessori should have been used all over the world exclusively for the education of non-handicapped children of normal ability, and that only some decades after its development did the idea occur to anyone to apply it to handicapped children as well. Through the German Council for Education, in 1967 I happened to meet a "mentally handicapped child" who was using Montessori materials in a Montessori nursery school in Frankfurt. This discovery led me to undertake a systematic study of the method and its materials, in the process of which it became apparent that here was an incredible and still unexploited resource for helping children with multiple and different types of handicaps.

After discovering the relevance of Montessori's educational theory to handicapped children, we set about trying to extend the foundations of the theory to develop a remedial approach and to utilize it for the benefit of children with multiple and different types of handicap.

KEYS TO THE WORLD

Therapeutic applications

The therapeutic potential of Montessori's theory lies primarily in its physiological approach to the senses. Learning by seeing, hearing, smelling, feeling, as well as through movement (kinaesthetic learning), is strongly encouraged in the Montessori approach by the material. The child assimilates auditory, visual, gustatory, tactile and olfactory impressions. By using sound boxes, colour charts, smell and taste boxes, and by feeling different shapes and degrees of roughness, he learns to grasp the meaning of things literally by taking hold of them. In this way he understands shape, size, colour, intensity, degree or quality. The child learns to understand contrasts or identity, and eventually the gentle gradations between the contrasts.

Working with the sensory material helps the child to understand what he sees, hears and touches. In sensorimotor learning, the child combines different impressions, and develops concepts. Only when these subprocesses are sufficiently developed is abstract thought possible.

Time and again we are struck by the children's joy in handling the Montessori materials, in ordering and arranging them, and experimenting with simple tasks, which are often repeated. The activities in every Montessori classroom, with the children working quietly and with concentration, are very impressive even for an outsider, and the learning of movement sequences, the carrying of materials and their combination reinforce the learning processes.

Decades ago, Maria Montessori described learning through movement as muscular memory, and kinaesthetic learning underlies many of the learning processes associated with Montessori materials, e.g. learning to write with sandpaper letters or using the figures of the geometric cabinet. On this basis, Montessori pupils do not become dyslexics, as has frequently been the case for years in a large percentage of our ordinary schools.

The significance of kinaesthetic learning also becomes obvious to the layman if we consider a task such as learning to skate, for example. Even learning five books on skating by heart will not allow the learner to move properly on the ice. This can only be learned by actively practising movements with the skates, until the necessary patterns of movement have finally been imprinted in the form of muscular memory by training coordination. Kinaesthetic learning has only a minor role in our ordinary schools, and the overemphasis on learning by reading and abstractions is a pointer to why, in terms of time and effort, our schools are inevitably less efficient compared to Montessori schools.

On the basis of these phenomena, it was not difficult to introduce paediatric and psychopaediatric knowledge into classical Montessori educational theory to provide help for children with multiple and different types of handicap. *The aims* may be briefly summarized as follows:

1. The treatment of disorders of speech and of perception,

2. The treatment of disorders in social development with the object of improving independence.

3. The social integration of disturbed or handicapped children, whatever the nature of their disorder, into the community of healthy children.

The social interaction between healthy and handicapped children promotes independence and sociability not only in the handicapped children, but also in the healthy ones.

Stages of Montessori remedial education

In terms of organization, the principle of Montessori remedial education comprises the following stages:

1. Individual therapy

In this stage, Montessori remedial education, working with the parents, and especially the mother, turns its attention to the individual handicapped child, for whose needs the classical Montessori materials have been adapted. This has led to the continuing development from practical experience with children of the remedial Montessori materials for children with multiple and different types of handicap. These materials are currently being subjected to continuous testing and improvement on children with different types of handicap.

2. Small group therapy

For this, the Montessori remedial teacher takes 2 or 3 handicapped children, firstly with, and later without, their parents, in order to practise social interaction with the children and the parents. The goal here is to make the children independent and to prepare them to live in a community.

3. Integrated education in the nursery school

Once the children have attained the necessary level of independence and sociability in their social development, they are educated in a nursery school together with healthy children. In Munich, a group size of 25 children proved successful, with 5 to 8 handicapped or potentially handicapped children, depending on the severity of the disorders or handicaps involved. These children should have various types of handicap (blindness, deafness, mental handicap, motor disabilities, behavioural problems etc.).

4. Integrated education at school

In the context of Montessori remedial education, the same principles have also been applied to integrated education at school, now both at primary and secondary school, in conjunction with special schools for educationally and mentally handicapped pupils.

In the model school, a class size of between 20 and 25 children proved successful, of which 5 to 7 children have multiple and different types of handicap. As in the nursery school, the type of handicap involved is less important than their level of social development, i.e. their independence and ability to work with other children. Children whose social development is impaired require greater attention from the teacher in smaller classes. This was the reason for officially establishing one school for educationally handicapped pupils and one school for mentally handicapped pupils, in accordance with Bavarian law. In practice, these separate schools do not exist, for the individual classes are next door to one another and exchange pupils even during lessons. Because all the children are taught in accordance with the official Bavarian syllabuses – each of which is different, with no pressure to do well, fear of school or overtly critical marking system – each child is free at any time to enter our school from the ordinary school system, or to move over successfully from our school into the ordinary school system, without incurring any disadvantage.

Integrated education in the context of Montessori's educational theory

The concept of integration has been common in educational theory at least since the report of the German Council for Education. Our daily papers still express astonishment if blind or physically handicapped children are occasionally taught together with non-handicapped children in some school or another.

The "Aktion Sonnenschein" experiment that I started almost 15 years ago in the Montessori schools of the Munich Paediatric Centre not only proves that Montessori's educational theory contains unique components of remedial value to children with multiple and different types of handicap, but also that no problems arise from teaching such children together with non-handicapped children in this system of education.

The organization and implementation of the project cannot be described in detail in this brief account. The reader is referred to the publications "Unser Montessori-Modell", "Die Montessori-Pädagogik und das behinderte Kind" and "Integrierte Erziehung gesunder Kinder mit mehrfach und verschieden behinderten Kindern – Schulversuch nach Maria Montessori der Aktion Sonnenschein in München".

KEYS TO THE WORLD

Successes in the integrated education of non-handicapped children in the Montessori system

The great success of the Montessori approach, especially in integrated education, is borne out by the fact that every year for more than 10 years about 21 children – half the pupils of the model classes – have moved to the Gymnasium (grammar school) after four years in school. Since the school is only licensed, but not accredited, by the state, they must first pass an entrance examination at a different school in subjects they are completely unfamiliar with. All the children have so far managed this easily and without any problems, and, where we have been able to keep track of their subsequent progress, have had no problems in holding their own at the Gymnasium.

Successes in the integrated education of handicapped children in the Montessori system

Our success with handicapped children can best be gauged from the results achieved by mentally handicapped, educationally handicapped and educationally difficult children during their period of education at our Montessori school:

– Out of 17 children classified as mentally handicapped on admission to school in 1974/1975, 2 children completed secondary school 8 years later, 7 finished as educationally handicapped, and only 8 finished as mentally handicapped children;

– Out of 16 children classified as educationally handicapped on admission to school at the same time, 8 completed secondary school normally and 8 finished as educationally handicapped;

– Out of 5 children classified as educationally difficult on admission to school, 4 completed secondary school normally, and one child finished as educationally handicapped.

These successes are corroborated by the fact that both assessment at the time of admission and the final examination were conducted by outside educational institutions.

BASIC IDEAS OF MONTESSORI'S EDUCATIONAL THEORY

Social learning

The success of integrated education within the framework of Montessori's educational theory can only be understood if we consider the significance of the young child's social development, defined as development towards independence and sociability, in practice towards working together with other children. Social learning is encouraged by helping and allowing others to help. With each act of helping, the child develops ever greater independence ("Only those who help become independent").

Even in normal circumstances, Montessori education encourages the development of independence in children in a special way, because it does not make use of year classes. In mixed-aged classes, the experienced pupil has the pleasure of helping the inexperienced child, who in turn learns to accept help from the experienced child.

These social interactions are further intensified in groups where different kinds of handicapped and non-handicapped children are taught together, because of the even greater differences in what the children can achieve, and because even handicapped children can help, depending on their abilities (the mentally handicapped child proudly pushing the physically handicapped child in a wheel-chair, the physically handicapped child helping the blind child with his reading).

Thus, via social development, integrated education also boosts cognitive performance, and children are given much greater encouragement than in schools which believe in providing children with special help through the use of performance groups or streaming (specialized special education).

Social development as the basis for developmental rehabilitation

As it currently stands, our research would suggest that the key to the success of integrated education using Montessori's educational theory lies in its promotion of social development.

174

Strong support for the development of the child's ability to work independently is already a normal part of Montessori education, and this process receives a boost from integrated education.

Scientific monitoring of our educational experiment, supported by the Federal Ministry for Education and Science, analyzed various aspects in more detail. Thus, in comparing groups with children of the same age from ordinary and special schools, my colleague Dietel found that children from our Montessori schools had significantly lower levels of exam nerves, manifest nerves and anxiety about school, as well as of practical physical ailments, than comparable children from ordinary state schools, including secondary schools and Gymnasiums.

In the programme of developmental rehabilitation, as it was founded 15 years ago in the Munich Paediatric Centre with the aim of utilizing the unique opportunities of early childhood development to rehabilitate children with congenital or early disorders or damage, Montessori education, including the form of Montessori remedial education developed in Munich, has a decisive role to play in the integration of those children who could not be rehabilitated by early treatment

into the family
into ordinary nursery school, and
into ordinary school.

This new approach is meanwhile starting to be accepted and practised not only in the Federal Republic of Germany, but also internationally.

Literature: Hellbrügge, Th.: *Unser Montessori-Modell. – Erfahrungen mit einem neuen Kindergarten und einer neuen Schule.* Kindler-Verlag, Munich 1977; – Id.: Montessori, M.: *Die Montessori-Pädagogik und das behinderte Kind.* Kindler, Munich 1978; – Papoušek, H., Papoušek, M.: Die Rolle der sozialen Interaktionen in der psychischen Entwicklung und Pathogenese von Entwicklungsstörungen im Säuglingsalter. In: G. Nissen (ed.), *Psychiatrie des Säuglings- und des frühen Kleinkindalters.* Verlag Hans Huber, Berne-Stuttgart-Vienna, p. 69–74, 1982; – Popper, K. R., Eccles, J. C.: *Das Ich und sein Gehirn.* Piper-Verlag, Munich-Zurich 1982.

BASIC IDEAS OF MONTESSORI'S EDUCATIONAL THEORY

Sources: (1) Karl Neise, Montessori und Heilpädagogik (1989 article); (2) Theodor Hellbrügge, Die Entdeckung der Montessori-Pädagogik für das behinderte Kind (1989 article).

IV

THE SECRET CENTRE

God and the Child

1939 (1) Mothers and fathers speak of "their child". They use the fact that they have brought the child "into the world" to justify this expression. But there is probably a deeper reason for the keen awareness the parents have of their responsibility to God for the child that he has entrusted to them. Even if it is true that the parents have helped to create the child, nobody will simply look upon that child as a product of man, a piece of property that he has made himself. The parents, and especially the mother, are keenly aware that they have only a minor part in the process of conception and birth, compared to the part played by nature. In reality, the germ-cells from which the child develops are not brought into being by an act of human will. The union of the germ-cells is much more the work of nature than of the parents, even if the latter must have performed an act of will as a necessary precondition. It is not the mother who is then responsible for the child's growth in her womb. The child achieves this growth through the power of the being that has been created within him. It is not the mother who performs the act of childbirth. This miraculous act is the doing of nature, while the mother has only a supporting role. And because God has ordained that conception should be like this, as well as development and birth, the parents feel such natural respect for the child, who has come to them in so miraculous a manner. And this respect increases still further when we realize another truth: The most important part of man, his soul, does not even come from man, but is created directly by God.

The idea that God has so mysteriously caused a being to grow within us and through us, while we have made only a modest contribution to the process, is likely to arouse great

177

respect. The works of God and nature always command greater respect than the things we create on our own. But we shall feel an even deeper reverence for the child when we fully understand how he appears to us after baptism. When a child has been baptized, and thus when his nature, which is corrupted by Original Sin, has been lowered into the grave of baptismal water and has arisen thence to new life with Christ and in the strength of the fruitful death of Christ, then we receive the child anew, who is now born again directly through God, who partakes of God with his own nature and is called a true son of God, and who is now to be in ever fuller possession of divine life. Whoever looks at the child in this way will tremble in awe, for in him he will see God. He will not see in the child the man-made possession with which he can do as he wishes. Rather he will be keenly aware that the child belongs to God much more than he does to himself, and owes his existence more to God than to himself, and that he has received the needy and defenceless child from God's hands, so that as an adult child of God he may guide this little child of God in accordance with divine will.

God reveals his will on the one hand through supernatural revelation, on the other through the nature of the living things which are part of his creation. But however God reveals his will and his desires, we must heed them. When we are faced with the task of helping the child to grow in accordance with nature and the supernatural, the first requirement is to seek reverently the path God wishes us to take.

God has given the child a nature of his own, and has thereby established certain laws of development, in both the physical and spiritual spheres. Whoever has responsibility for the child's normal development must therefore follow these laws. If we deviate from them, we shall lose the direction that God provides to guide the child, for we are not then in touch with the laws which God himself has established.

If we discover these laws governing the development of the child, then we discover the spirit and the wisdom of God who is at work within the child. We must respect the objective needs of the child as something which God himself has instructed us to satisfy. This is the true spirit of education, for it means that divine wisdom itself is embodied through the actions of teachers and educators. If in the voice of nature we recognize the voice of God telling us to help the child, then we shall always be prepared to fulfil these needs. We shall then realize that in this way we are lending ourselves to God's plans, and that we have a part in God's work in the child. We shall not then consider it a tiresome obligation selflessly to accommodate the demands of the child who is entrusted to our care, but shall see it as fulfilling the wishes of God, who reveals himself in the child. Only the recognition of God in his laws and in the expression of his will in children actually enables us to live for the child and to renounce ourselves.

Among those who have departed from the faith, there is sometimes great emphasis on reverence for the child. But true reverence for the child is only possible – in view of our egotism and desire for domination and power – if we honour God in the child. Whoever does not believe in God, who is the beginning and the end of all things, and whoever considers man himself as the supreme being, inexorably succumbs to an attitude of arrogance towards the child, and under the guise of concern is bound to begin a veritable struggle with him, in order to make him conform to his own imagined model and ideal. What we observe in public life can also be seen in education: where the will of God is no longer the guiding principle, the powerful treat the weak as creatures without rights, because in such a situation they are themselves the law-makers who decide the fate of the underdog. Even if there is no arbitrary abuse of power in an environment without faith, reverence is violated in another way. We shall then only respect those things in the child which can casily be seen, and we shall reduce him to a creature unfamiliar with the ideal of objective perfection. It would be hard to conceive of the child with less respect than by assuming that his nature has no demands of its own. True respect presupposes the recognition of an ideal that God wishes to realize in the child. There is an ideal not only in nature, but also in the supernatural realm, and just as the education of physical and spiritual life is nothing other than working together with the natural forces of development, so super-natural education is nothing other than working together with the grace of God. Filled with awe at the grace of God in the child, it must be our constant aim to guide the child to place himself fully under the influence of the formative power of the grace of God. Now supernatural growth is linked to the use of the means which God himself has ordained, the most important of which are the sacraments and prayer. It is quite contrary to the laws of supernatural development to equate the means of natural education with those of supernatural education.

But even if it is true that grapes (supernature) cannot be gathered from thorns (nature), it should not be concluded that supernatural development is equally certain in all natural conditions. The teacher must therefore ascertain exactly which internal and external circumstances and con-ditions are most advantageous to the child, so that children are all the more susceptible to supernatural influence and to vigorous and continual involvement with the grace of God.

Deeper respect for the nature of the child will also bring greater success in educating him in supernatural life. Those who do not understand that the child perceives the truths of the faith somewhat differently to adults, and that he has other ways of expressing his trust in and love of God, will provide him with inappropriate guidance. The child must also enter into supernatural life in his own way. Even to God, the child must be a child! This is what God himself wishes, which is why he has made him a child. Reverence for the nature of the child, which God himself has ordained, obliges us to observe closely the conditions in which children can turn more fully towards God. Even in relation to the en-lightening and compelling grace of God himself, the child often reveals his striving after God.

This discovery ought to make us very happy, and after-wards, prompted as we are by our reverence for this manifest desire, we must do everything we possibly can to create conditions better suited to satisfying this desire on the part of the child in an appropriate manner. We shall probably need to create a completely different environment, and a complete readjustment of our personal attitudes will also certainly be required. But the results that ensue will readily compensate us for such sacrifices, if the child is given the opportunity to live his own full religious life, because this life will then put down much deeper roots in the soul, and is much less dependent on prompting by teachers. The religious life of the small child will also give so much more stimulation to the religious life of the adult, especially since the latter will gain in truth and reality. When we have learned to respect children's own religious life, and when we understand its great seriousness, then it will no longer occur to us to smile if a small child quite spontaneously bestows a consoling kiss on the image of Christ on the Cross, or offers him a child's present. Then there is no way that we shall reveal, either by what we say or the way we look at him, that actions like these strike us as peculiar. Neither with admiration, nor praise, nor encouragement shall we interfere with the development of this fine spontaneity, once we have learned to recognize similar phenomena as natural forms of expression at a certain stage of the child's life.

If we gain greater respect for the rights and needs of the child, then our affection for him will also change in a particular way. Our severity, our imperiousness, our arbitrary acts of restraint, which are due more to our bad temper than to the pursuit of any particular educational objective on our part, will disappear. We will know better how to follow the practical advice of Saint Paul to the Ephesians, "And you, fathers, do not provoke your children to anger" (Eph. 6,4). And when we read in the encyclical of Pope Pius XI concerning Christian education that such provocation to anger "is due above all to the fact that parents have too little patience to tolerate the spontaneity and inherent liveliness of their children", then we shall have greater respect the child's nature in accordance with the Holy Father's admonition. We shall also learn to overcome our vanity, which so likes to boast of what our children achieve, even in the manner of prayer, for their natural simplicity will be too sacred for us to violate. We shall beware of the impatience that forces children to do things that are still beyond their abilities, giving rise to fears of failure which will lead to attitudes of inhibitedness, fear and shyness. We might say, "Have the patience of the Virgin Mary, mother of the child of God, who knew how to wait humbly for the miracles of the son".

If reverence for the child were more common, we would take care not to do in our impatience what children can do very well themselves at their own somewhat slower pace, and which they would do with the greatest of pleasure. Respect for the laws of child development would keep us from urging children on at full speed to behave like adults at an earlier age, for, in order to become truly adult, it is necessary for a child to pass properly through the natural stages of childhood.

But respect for the rights of the child to advance step by step along the path of development could also lead us to keep the child at a stage that he naturally wants to leave behind. It is quite out of keeping with the natural needs of a seven year old child for him to be cuddled like a little baby of just a few months. Such tendencies derive from a well-known need on the part of the adult, but are no more admissible for that. We want to keep the child in a state of needy and infantile dependency, so that we feel permanently indispensable. Lack of respect for the laws of child development often leads the adult to behave just as he pleases towards the child. The somewhat pathetic complaint "My son is growing apart from me and has less need of me, I am losing him" shows that it can be quite difficult not to hold on to a child as one's own possession.

Respect for these needs of development is so absolutely necessary, because in early infancy children are especially vulnerable, both physically and psychologically. Anomalies and diseases are very apt to develop at this time which make it impossible, or at least very difficult, for the child to attain full psychological and physical development. Only recently have we understood this fact, and developments in this area were the same as with the concept of Original Sin.

Original Sin, which is a consequence of mankind's first fall, aroused less concern at the time of its origins than it did in the following centuries, when man had been set free from it. We are therefore faced with a contrast which appears to contradict all human logic: little interest in Original Sin in the era when it was of importance, with all its consequences; and much anxiety about Original Sin precisely in the era of redemption, when it had lost much of its influence. In the field of education, we are faced with a similar contrast. In the past, when civilization was too exclusively founded upon and geared towards the adult, the sad consequences of this educational offence became apparent, this error which had been perpetrated against the very origins of mankind, namely the child. But at the time, people were less concerned with this first error, devoting little attention to this first mistake, this educational offence against the beginnings of mankind in the child, which brought so much misery in its wake!. But now, in an era when the child is being freed from the consequences of this error, because educators are becoming wiser, much attention is being devoted to this educational offence. The result of this intense interest has been to show clearly that our troubles, our psychological difficulties, originate above all in the period of childhood. According to new research, the origins of physical and mental illnesses, character imbalances and vital degeneration can be traced back primarily to early childhood life. There is a growing conviction that anomalies and abnormalities are largely due to habit and neglect or arbirary treatment, or to demanding too much or too little of the child in his early years. And since psychology, educational theory and psychiatry are based on this conviction, they are turning their attention to the child in a way that was unknown in the past.

This offence against the early stage of life, which appears to us as so delicate, ought to induce us to ask with great respect what nature, and therefore God, demands of us.

BASIC IDEAS OF MONTESSORI'S EDUCATIONAL THEORY

It is really not the aim of our new educational theory to champion the idea of having to ask the child "what he likes". But on the basis of our respect for the child's right to a sound education, he tells us what his real needs are, so that he can grow up normally and fully develop the powers which God himself has given him.

The realization that both in his nature and in his supernature the child has preserved God's true Creation better than all others will make it easier for us to show this reverence. Let us therefore respect the child, who in his nature as in his supernatural being reveals divine Creation in still more unspoilt form.

The respect in which we should hold the child, we demand in the name of the divine friend of children.

We do not find much in the Gospel about Jesus's thoughts and attitudes as far as children are concerned. But what the Holy Scriptures do tell us only serves to deepen our reverence for the child still further. We mean above all Jesus's harsh attitude towards adults who cause offence to children, an almost violent attitude, such as when he turned against the adult in the temple who was desecrating the very house of God. He said to those who offend against the innocence of children and desecrate the holy temple in this way, "But whoever leads astray one of these little ones who put faith in me, it is more beneficial for him to have hung around his neck a millstone and to be sunk in the wide open sea. Woe to the world because of the offences" (Mt 18,6–7).

Christ not only addresses a strong warning to those who offend against little children, he will not suffer anyone of them to be despised: "See to it that you do not despise one of these little ones" (Mt 18,10).

What disdain is often revealed by the use of the word "childishness". With such a word we seek to excuse all types of discourtesy and neglect towards children.

In Jesus's mind there is no reason to see children as "merely childish". Jesus objects to undervaluing them in this way, and the reason he gives for not despising them is impressive: "For I say to you that their angels always behold the face of my Father who is in heaven" (Mt 18,10).

THE SECRET CENTRE

With these words, Jesus wishes to impress on us the importance of the following idea: "Have deep reverence for these little ones, because God esteems them highly and gives them their own angel to protect them in heaven".

This respect which he, Jesus, demands, is also made apparent in his own behaviour. When he was setting forth his great teaching on marriage to the learned and distinguished Hebrews, some children came close to him. The apostles would not let them near, and wanted to send them away. These children had no business there, while Jesus was speaking with the distinguished Hebrews – or so the apostles probably thought. But the divine friend of children had other ideas, as he made clear to the apostles. He appeared angry and said, "Let the children alone, and stop hindering them from coming to me" (Mt 19,14).

And the reason? "For the kingdom of heaven belongs to suchlike ones". And Jesus then embraced the little ones, and as a sign of his blessing he put his hands upon them. And in the Gospel according to St. Mark we further read these words of Jesus, "Truly I say to you, whoever does not receive the kingdom of heaven like a young child, will not enter into it" (Mk 10,15–16). The simplicity with which the child receives the mysteries of God is held up as an example for our spiritual attitude, and in this sense the child is put forward as a guide who can unwittingly show us the way.

On another occasion, the apostles made it known that they aspired to a privileged place in the kingdom which Christ would found. When they asked Jesus which of them would be the greater, he called a child to him and set him in their midst and said, "Unless you turn around and become as young children, you will not enter into the kingdom of heaven" (Mt 18,3). And elsewhere it is added, "Whoever is the lesser one among all of you is the only one that is great" (Lk 9,48).

Respect for another becomes even more apparent if there is no feeling of superiority, but rather of equality. And thus God preferred to enter the world as a child and to pass through all the stages of a child's life. Therefore whoever

185

despises children because they are "merely children", reveals a lack of respect.

The child exerts a particular influence on us here in his capacity as a child, and we also see the child in the Infant Jesus. Nobody will deny that the festival of the birth of Christ, which celebrates the same Christ who died and rose again, has a different effect on us than Easter. For instance, at Christmas it is the child who dominates us. At Christmas we are overcome by the weakness of children, by their state of helplessness and their delicateness. We then become meek and kind. The all-powerful child, who takes on a weak appearance, has a disarming effect on us. It is no surprise that the shepherds tending their flocks should have experienced the glory of "peace on earth" of which the angels who had descended from heaven were singing.

Jesus probably often speaks to us even more movingly as a child than as an adult. When we think of the Christ child, we can learn to put aside our arrogant attitudes towards the child. In the reverent power of love, which we sometimes view as weakness, we shall then see the true symbol of our attitude as adults. The means through which the child influences us, his reverent and trusting love, will then also be our great strength in the field of education.

In imitation of our great master, we shall not allow ourselves to be dominated by the urge for admiration and power, but by reverence for the figure of Christ in the child, who with our assistance should grow until he attains the full potential of his personality.

Christ once said some words in which he virtually equated himself with children: "Whoever receives this child in my name receives me too, and whoever receives me receives him also that sent me forth" (Lk 9,48).

If we see Christ and the Father in the child, our reverence for the little ones will be profound and sacred. And, as preparers of the way for Christ in the child, we may sincerely say in the words of Saint John, "That one (he) must go on increasing, but I must go on decreasing" (Joh 3,30).

Source: (1) *Kinder, die in der Kirche leben,* p. 233–244.

V

THE ADVENTURE OF A LIFE IN THE SERVICE OF THE CHILD

(by G. Schulz-Benesch)

Maria Montessori was born in 1870 in Chiaravalle near Ancona. She grew up in a middle-class home – her father was a civil servant at the time of the Risorgimento, and a relative of her mother was a well-known priest and scholar – and showed remarkable talent at an early age. Her parents wanted their daughter to become a teacher, but this was not at all what Maria wanted. Since the ordinary secondary schools where pupils were prepared for college did not admit girls at that time, Montessori attended a "technical school", a kind of secondary or grammar school (with a scientific bias). One reason for this in particular was Montessori's great aptitude for mathematics, and indeed it was her intention to study the subject. Quite suddenly, however, she changed her plans, and later on she would occasionally speak of the reasons for this. One day in a street in Rome – to where the Montessori family had since moved – she had seen a poor woman sitting on a step with a small child in her lap, and the child was holding a red strip of cardboard. This was the moment when the decision to study medicine quite suddenly "came" to her. This is an unusual choice of words, to say that the decision "came", but this is exactly the way things happened in Montessori's life. For all her remarkable intellectual gifts, the important decisions in her life were typically taken in the context of real-life situations, on the basis of intuition. Her friend Anna Maccheroni tells us, "... she herself asked, 'Why?' ... she intimated to us that strange things happen to us to lead us to a goal we are unaware of ..."

At that time, of course, women were not allowed to study medicine, and her application was promptly turned down by the Italian minister of education. The young Montessori went to see him and, when he had informed her of all the reasons for the refusal, she said, "Your Excellency, I *shall* study medicine!" In addition to her mathematical and scientific talents and her intuitive behaviour, this incident shows a third feature of her character: tenacity of will.

Well, Montessori did become the first female medical student and the first woman doctor in Italy, which is why she was often simply known as the "Dottoressa", that is the "woman doctor". There is much that could be told about her student years. Just think of dissection classes, for example, where, being the only girl among the male students, for reasons of decorum she was always sent alone (that is, with only a chaperon) to the mortuary, which as a rule she could only visit at night. She endured all the problems of the frontline struggle for the emancipation of women at the time. Montessori also had contacts with feminist organizations, something that would otherwise hardly have been possible.

More important in her life at this time and later, however, were quite different, personal experiences and painful events which drew her increasingly towards children and their multifarious problems, and which eventually led her to her life's work.

In 1896, she became an intern in the psychiatric department of the paediatric clinic of the University of Rome. Here she had a shocking experience. The first time she went to visit the feeble-minded children, she found the nurse highly abusive about the little ones, saying they were all dirty and greedy. When the young doctor enquired further, it emerged that the main reason for the nurse thinking this was that the children would play on the floor with the bread they were given, make it into shapes, and then eat it, all dirty as it was. Montessori looked around the room. In the entire children's ward, there was nothing, absolutely nothing except for beds.

Thus the poor little children would play with the only thing that they were given, their bread. Maria Montessori was deeply affected by this, she was shocked to realize that the children were being abused by a failure adequately to encourage their urge for activity. She sought to help the children.

In the process, she came across the work of the French doctor Séguin. Around the middle of the 19th century, the latter had developed a system of education which was designed to assist the development of feeble-minded children by means of sensory exercices using didactic materials. Montessori took up this preliminary work when she herself started teaching feeble-minded children in 1898. She further developed Séguin's material, and the successes she achieved in teaching caused a sensation. In a state examination, the children at her institute showed themselves to be equal to ordinary elementary school pupils in spelling and writing. But Montessori wrote: "While everybody was busy admiring the progress of my idiots, I examined the reasons why children in our state schools achieve such low levels of performance …". She first succeeded in utilizing her experiences for the education of normal children of pre-school age in her first "Casa dei Bambini", which she opened in 1907 in the working-class San Lorenzo district of Rome. In this "Children's House" in the slums, Montessori developed her method of infant education. She soon extended her educational work to include the primary school level up to the age of 12, so that the essential features of the system known as "Montessori Education" were in place by around the start of the First World War. It spread rapidly throughout many countries, as did her writings.

According to Montessori herself, the origins of her entire work lie in her experience of the "polarization of attention" which she encountered in her first Children's House. There, she saw a little girl of about three years of age, completely absorbed in a "sensory exercise", namely the so-called solid insets (roughly comparable to the weight-trays of the old type of kitchen scales). She refused to be deflected from her concentrated activity, either when Montessori placed her

189

upon the table together with her chair, or when she got the other children to sing. Montessori counted 44 repetitions of the exercise, and when the child stopped, she did so quite independently of any distractions around her. She was not tired, but "looked happily around her, as if … awaking from a refreshing sleep …"

This phenomenon completely contradicted her previous "belief in the characteristic instability of attention in young children …" Yet from now on she was to observe over and over again this "polarization of attention" and its surprising effects, which led to a "normalization" of the child, as she put it: "… all that was disorderly and fluctuating in the soul of the child seemed to be organizing itself into a spiritual creation, the surprising characteristics of which are reproduced in every individual child". From now on, Montessori's work was determined by the sensational successes which were achieved in education and teaching using the phenomenon she described, and which were confirmed by innumerable witnesses. This phenomenon, which was later often described as the "Montessori phenomenon", and which Montessori herself simply calls "the discovery of the child", is the basis of her entire work: "… from now on it was my endeavour to seek exercise materials which facilitated the child's concentration, and moreover I scrupulously sought to determine the type of environment which offers the best external conditions for this concentration." She considered that any such study must involve the observation of normal children who feel themselves to be free. On the basis of these tireless investigations and experiments, Montessori now began to organize the Children's House, the "prepared environment", a place that held out a constant invitation to unconstrained activity, a world of "obliging situations".

The whole establishment is suited to the needs of the child. All the furniture, household utensils etc. are appropriate for the size and physical strength of a young child. Numerous "exercises of practical life" are introduced. Examples include: washing one's hands, cleaning metals, tending flowers, feeding animals, preparing meals. But there are also social exercises, manual skills, pottery making, rhythmical exercises and other collective activities.

As with the "exercises of practical life", the principle of free choice, i.e. in practice largely individual activity, also applies to the use of the "sensory materials". These are firstly the aforementioned solid insets of various sizes, in which the children are encouraged to remove and replace the cylinders in a wooden block. Then there are a set of cubes with edges of decreasing length, a set of rectangular solids of decreasing cross-section, a set of rods of decreasing length. These represent various dimensions, and invite the children to arrange them in the form of a "tower", "steps" etc. In addition we find objects for tactile exercises, boards with sandpaper glued to them representing different degrees of asperity, and a small collection of different kinds of material which can be distinguished by touch. There are similar materials for colour, weight, noise, sound, smell, taste etc., besides combined sensory exercises. Usually the first step with the sensory materials is to establish identities, then to distinguish increasingly subtle gradations.

All the exercises are introduced by the teacher, and offer the opportunity for self-supervision. Observing children choosing their own activities leads Montessori to the concept of "sensitive periods", periods of particular sensitivity to certain impressions, as for instance with the strong impulse to learn language. Montessori identifies such periods in many tendencies, even in a way in activities associated with the learning of cultural techniques and other concerns of education. Accordingly, she calls for the observation and analysis of the stages of education and teaching which are regarded as typical of particular levels though varying on an individual basis. This was one more reason for extending her work to children of school age.

With her extensive teaching materials, she takes up the preparation by means of sensory materials without the child's knowledge. Montessori insists on having the Children's House and school in *one* building, with open doors between the Children's House and the school and between the individual classes. According to her instructions, these classes, which should contain no more than about 40 and not less than 20–25 children, each comprise about three years. In some countries, Montessori schools soon extended as far as the final year of primary school, in Holland at first to university entrance level. In work with older children and young people, free work in groups and collective teaching of the children play a larger role than before alongside individual activity. For young people, Montessori called for a temporary period of residence in a kind of boarding-school in the country.

But let us now return to the astonishingly rapid and widespread dissemination of Montessori's ideas and suggestions.

How did this come about?

The real reason lies mainly in her development of practical educational work, not primarily in her theories. People were so astonished, even staggered, by her educational successes in the first Children's House in Rome and then in the other Children's Houses and the schools that soon followed, that a veritable educational pilgrimage began from all over the world. Everybody wanted to see the educational "miracle". At first it was mainly English and Americans, but very soon also people from Australia, South America and Japan. Interest in Europe came from people of all nations, but especially from Austrians, Germans, Dutch, French, Belgians, Spanish, Hungarians and Russians. Many of Montessori's visitors urged her to speak about her work, and so she held her first training course in Città di Castello in 1909. It was around the same time that Montessori's Children's House received a visit from a taciturn Italian officer, the husband of one of her patrons. It is relevant to an understanding of subsequent events for us to listen in on the conversation that followed this visit, with the help of notes made by a witness, her friend Anna Maria Maccheroni. After he had stayed a long time, Maria Montessori finally asked the taciturn officer what he thought of the Children's House.

"'Have you written a book?' he asked laconically.

'A book? ... no!'

'But you might die, and all this would be lost!'

The Dottoressa enjoyed good health.

The baron told her she should write a book straight away, and invited her to the beautiful Villa Volkonsky, where she was offered every comfort to write in the open, in the beautiful, verdant park.

Elisabetta Ballerini went with her.

Twenty days later, the manuscript was ready ... The next day, the baron took the train to Città di Castello, where he was well known, and there he gave the manuscript to a printer's, not a publisher, with the order to print it sentence for sentence, without altering even a single comma.

This was the origin of her first book of 'The Method'".

Elsa Ochs's[1] description of the genesis of the "method", which follows Montessori's personal account, confirms and supplements Maccheroni's description: "For two years, Dr. Montessori had worked quietly in the Children's Houses, but even then, as she said herself, it would not have occurred to her to write a book. But little by little visitors came to Italy from all over the world, and especially America, to see the work of the Dottoressa, who eventually yielded to pressure from her friends and set down the principles of the method in writing ... When the last page proof finally lay stapled neatly on the author's desk, she felt relieved of a great burden. She took the whole volume and threw it playfully into the air, so that the pages fluttered apart and flew around the room in confusion. After great effort, Mrs Montessori and her pupils managed to rearrange the work, but she did not regret what she had done, for, as she herself relates, this impulsive act seemed to symbolize her need to consign that period, which was now over, entirely to the past".

These comments are remarkably characteristic of Montessori. She has already been working for years, is deeply moved by her discoveries and already has a considerable following – and only then does her first, later so celebrated book appear, quite by chance and almost as an afterthought. And learned and not so learned authors, educationalists, psychologists,

---

[1] Who emigrated from Germany to America during the Nazi period.

philosophers and theologians write profound criticisms of formulations which first arose on a beautiful day in the park and, with the aid of various preparatory notes, were assembled into a bulky volume within 20 days. Is it any surprise if they contained occasional errors, if various short-comings, unpolished passages, contradictions or exaggerations were found in the work of a Catholic doctor trained in the positivist tradition of the time, and who, with a brilliant and practical talent for education but a certain disdain for philosophy, tried to do and to describe her work? It is of some relevance that to this very day this first book has remained Montessori's best-known work, and in some countries her only well-known work.

By the time of the First World War, it was already available in the following languages: Italian, English (and an American edition), French, German, Polish, Russian, Japanese, Romanian, Spanish, Dutch, Danish and Chinese.

As a result of the numerous visitors she received, and now also through her writings, Montessori's educational theory was already well-known everywhere by the time of the First World War. Her work and writings were less methodically and theoretically orientated, so it was important that she passed on her educational theory in personal courses of instruction. She gave up her medical calling, abandoned an excellent medical practice and gave up a university career she had already started, in order to devote her life entirely to children.

We must now tell of a fateful coincidence of private and professional circumstances that helps us to understand the origins of the Montessori system.

Her friend Anna Maccheroni said, "The 'method' was born of sorrow", when she told me the precise circumstances in Rome in 1957. I also heard the same phrase elsewhere, from within Montessori's immediate circle, her son Mario among others. The impetus for her work with the children of the first Children's House in San Lorenzo basically goes back to some very depressing personal experiences, in particular to the unhappy circumstances connected with her position as an unmarried mother – her child only returned to his mother in early adolescence. And her takeover of the San Lorenzo Children's House is indirectly connected with the pressures that had led her to discontinue her work at the Scuola Ortofrenica some time previously, where she had been working with the child's father. It was thus not so much design as fate which led her, as she was once to say later, "by chance" to San Lorenzo and to her "discoveries" there. These tribulations could greatly help to explain the original context of her new work, but more especially could also help us to understand her repeated affirmation of the gift-like nature, the unexpectedness of the "discovery" at San Lorenzo. It did not involve the growth of an intended "seed", but the discovery of a "treasure" in her field of activity there.

Even in old age, Montessori repeatedly emphasizes the importance of this first Children's House in connection with her "discovery": "… this first institution of mine is important and we owe a great debt of gratitude to these first children, for without their example no one would have known all about this." She speaks frankly of this Children's House as "the first beginnings of my work". And she indicates this change of perspective and method when speaking of the initial "obstacles which lay between myself and the child": "The greatest obstructions were due to my own development, the long duration of my studies and my complete devotion to the learning of the early years".

To this early period of her more widely known educational work belongs a decision of significance to the development of Montessori's educational theory. Montessori, as a religious and "radical" woman in the positive sense of the word, wondered whether she ought to devote herself and all her work specially to God. She contemplated the idea of founding a religious order that would be dedicated to education.

I have investigated these somewhat obscure circumstances, and was able to learn from Montessori's family and from her old and close friend in Rome, Anna Maccheroni, that on the advice of Father Tacchi Venturi SJ, Montessori refrained from carrying out her plan. Both Mario Montessori and Anna Maccheroni reported the Father's advice by saying that he had told Maria Montessori that her ideas ought not to remain restricted to a particular group through the founding of an order, but that she should "give them to the world". From then on, Montessori followed this advice in her manifest efforts to avoid obstacles to the acceptance of her educational theory.

Here, then, is an important key to understanding why any personal profession of religious belief only comes through indirectly in Montessori's general writings on education, a fact which, incidentally, has led many Catholics in particular to doubt Montessori's religiousness. Of course, readers such as these did not know Montessori personally, and were no more familiar with her writings on religious education, for which she had become better known since the period of the First World War. Yet on the other hand, very many liberals and socialists as well as members of all the other great religious communities of the world took up Montessori's ideas. However positive this was in some respects, it led to a situation where, in Germany for instance, even discerning Christians only very gradually recognized the potential for a new type of education contained in Montessori's theory, while the publication of Montessori's writings was influenced to such a great extent by her other supporters that, for example, all obvious religious passages were omitted from her second major work.

Montessori's writings on religious education were simply not translated at all into German. Thus, by the National Socialist era, there were socialist and liberal groups using Montessori educational theory, but only the beginnings of Catholic involvement.

In many other countries, things were quite different, as for instance in Italy, where the recognition given to Montessori's work by Popes Pius X and Benedict XV contributed greatly to its popularity.

Soon after the National Socialist takeover in Germany came the first persecution of individual Montessori educationalists. Two socialist Montessori teachers disappeared in Berlin, while in Aachen the leader of the Catholic Montessori teachers, Helene Helming, was banned from teaching because of her extensive international connections. Montessori schools were closed, because the teachers opposed the application of "Jewish quotas"[2] to their schools. In the end, Montessori education was completely banned in Germany. The Gestapo had intervened. In a square in Berlin, Montessori's books were burned. A leading socialist Montessori educationalist, Clara Grunwald, was later murdered in the Holocaust.

These events are directly related to Montessori's internationalism and her universally appealing openness. It is interesting to observe that her ideas were welcomed everywhere except in those places where common humanity itself had been violated and freedom had been suppressed. Thus Montessori education thrived in some cities in Soviet Russia, but only until the hard-line policies of the Stalin years. The revolutionaries who spoke honestly of freedom in the spirit of Tolstoy were able to make use of a method of education which involved responsibility in freedom such as Montessori practised, but not a dictatorship. In the end it was anthropological shortcomings in totalitarian ideologies which destroyed Montessori's educational theory in the areas they controlled. "Race" in the case of the National Socialists: "Heredity is a word like chloroform – it dulls the mind", Montessori had said in 1933. And in the case of Communism, "a social detail", a single aspect, had been made the general foundation "in a society which as yet has not completely evolved". "The question of humanity", however, had to be placed "on a universal basis", the nature of man and the conditions of his development.

It is clear: neither "natural predisposition" nor "environment" suffice to define man – there is also the "directive of free choice" (W. Flitner).

In her last newspaper article in 1952, Montessori wrote, "Free choice was the first of the priorities in my plan of

---

[2] The percentage of pupils from German-Jewish marriages still permitted in individual schools in the early days of Nazi Germany.

education ... we ought not to wait until he (the child) reaches the age of discretion before explaining the importance and dignity of freedom to him! ... Freedom of choice leads to human dignity".

In Italy as well, events took a similar turn in the end. This was where Montessori had started, and at first her work had achieved positive results. Even before the First World War, she had accepted invitations to travel abroad, including to America, where she was greeted with confetti and described as "The most interesting woman of Europe". While her ideas were gaining ground here and were being analyzed by American educationalists, we find Montessori in Spain, where from her books Catholic priests had come to see her educational theory as essentially Christian, and had invited her to work with them. Here Montessori also took the opportunity to broaden the scope of her work in extensive experiments to include religious instruction. In Barcelona she founded the "House of Children in the Church" in conjunction with the Church authorities, and for the first time practised a form of religious education centred directly around the reality of Christian life, i.e. chiefly around the liturgy. This work was first described at the Liturgical Congress in Montserrat (1915). In 1916, Montessori took up residence in Barcelona.

But the Fascist upheaval was soon to take place in Italy, and with it Montessori's educational theory experienced its first difficulties in the educationalist's native land. Influential Socialists had supported Montessori education as much as the Church authorities. Soon we again find Italian socialists living as émigrés abroad, and especially in Russia. There was a threat that Montessori education would be banned. Montessori succeeded in obtaining an audience with Mussolini, where she spoke with him about children. At the end of her lengthy visit to the "Duce", she emerged with the absolutely astonishing news that Mussolini had become honorary president of the Italian Montessori Society.

However, this success, which was indicative of Montessori's personal influence, did not entirely achieve the results that had been hoped for. In fact the Fascists made increasing efforts to represent the world-famous education-alist as an example of Italian national achievement. After trying to reach agreement with them, Montessori eventually turned her back on the regime. From her permanent home in Barcelona, she continued to work hard to further the interests of children in modern society. In 1936, Montessori education was also suppressed in Italy, on the pretext that Montessori was an Anglophile. She was later asked in this connection whether she had changed her nationality, and what her national affiliations now were. Her answer was a fine example both of her basic philosophy and of her much admired eloquence: "… my country is a star which turns around the sun and is called the Earth".

Even in Spain, where she held many international courses, and where, especially in Catalonia, there were numerous Catholic as well as non-denominational Children's Houses and schools, there were set-backs. At first the Catalan government adopted a tough anticlerical line, with the result that Montessori's "House of Children in the Church" had to be closed. Montessori poignantly expressed her sorrow at this event when she wrote:

"The course of 'modern Catalan culture' considers itself 'progressive' when it shows religion its place, which is not the first place that it deserves … in order to give 'freedom' to ideas which have already had their day in other countries.

This leads to the infiltration of a misunderstood 'breadth' of ideas which blurs them all and builds up tension that will erupt in storms in the future.

This is unfortunately the new so-called social reform move-ment. Why did God allow us to be driven by a storm from the first 'House of Children in the Church'? Perhaps so that we would be prompted to continue to advance in our apostleship: Go forth and teach all nations … these are the powerful and heartening words of Jesus Christ".

Subsequent developments proved Montessori right. The expected "storms" did occur, even if only more than ten years later. The educationalist was still able to continue holding

199

her courses in Barcelona, and could still undertake international travel from there. In the 1920's, Montessori is to be found above all in Holland, England and South America, but time and again we meet her on her courses in Catalonia. Some German émigrés were ultimately able to escape via Barcelona at an international course in 1933.

In these years between the two great wars, Montessori made a good many important friends. Thus she struck up a warm relationship with Gandhi and Nehru. Adolphe Ferrière was an admirer of her work, and she got to know Rabindranath Tagore. But in her own intuitive manner, Montessori sensed a dark future threatening Europe and the world. In 1932 she gave a lecture on "Education and Peace" at the "Bureau International d'Éducation" in Geneva, which was then working with the League of Nations, in which she made the following pronouncement: "The crisis we are experiencing is not the sort of upheaval that marks the passage from one historical period to another. It can be compared only to one of those biological or geological epochs in which new, higher, more perfect forms of life appeared, as totally new conditions on earth came about.

If we do not appreciate this situation for what it is, we shall find ourselves confronting a universal cataclysm ... If man, in his ignorance ... uses the energies of space for the purpose of destroying himself, he will soon attain that goal, for the energies now at his disposal are immeasurable and accessible to everyone, at all times and in every corner of the earth".

From that time until the outbreak of World War II, she fought at numerous conferences and congresses, especially in Great Britain, Holland, Belgium and Scandinavia, on behalf of peace, which she felt to be closely bound up with education.

But now a series of terrible events began. Let us follow Montessori as she made her way through those years of war and revolution.

The outbreak of the Spanish Civil War led to increasing extremism among Socialist groups in Catalonia. It was often enough to be an Italian or a professed Catholic to be in the greatest danger, Montessori's son said of this period in Barcelona. Montessori was both. When the steps of heavily armed militiamen were heard approaching her house, everyone thought this was the end. However, the soldiers did not force an entry, but did something to the wall of the house. When they had left, the residents found an inscription emblazoned on the wall, saying "Spare this house – a friend of little children lives here". Maria Montessori then managed to escape from Barcelona on board a British warship. She turned up on the English ship with only what she could carry in her hands. She was cheerful, a friend reports, and, though without any belongings, considered it an adventure to eat heartily from tins.

In England, she arrived at exactly the right time to open a local course which had just been set up. A little later, we encounter her working in Holland, where she proposed to settle, being unable to return to Italy. A Montessori centre was created in Laren, and major new plans were discussed. Montessori wanted to take up an invitation to go to India, and Tagore was already looking forward to her visit. She even made her departure. It was shortly after the outbreak of the Second World War, late 1939. Soon afterwards, German troops invaded Holland – she was now unable to return there. A little later, Italy declared war on France and England. In India, Montessori was interned as an Italian national and spent a long time in detention.

Although Montessori was already seventy years old, this period failed to discourage her. Internment was relaxed, and by the time Montessori returned to Holland in 1949 she had built up a thriving Montessori educational system in India. Indeed, the training courses which she ran during her years in India were also attended by Pakistanis and in particular by Ceylonese. It is not long before we also find Montessori Children's Houses in Ceylon. A start was also made in Pakistan.

An important part of her late work which she had planned in England during the 1930s was completed in India – the conception of "Cosmic Education" with which she aimed to prepare young people, and especially 6–12 year olds, for their task as custodians and joint creators of the world.

Immediately after the War, Montessori visited Italy once more, where she was given a tumultuous reception and received numerous honours as the Italian who, in the words of the greeting of the Constitutional Assembly, "has honoured the name of Italy all over the world".

She gave courses in various countries and was finally to return to Holland in 1949.

On a spring day in 1952, this still sprightly woman of nearly 82 years of age sent a greeting on the occasion of the founding of the English "Catholic Montessori Guild", in which we read:

"Never, as at this moment, has the Christian Faith needed the earnest endeavour of those who profess it ... Children are sent to us as a rain of souls, as a wealth and a promise that can always be fulfilled; but that needs our efforts to help in bringing about that fulfilment ... Take then as aid in your task, in all humility and faith, the 'all-powerful children' (Benedict XV); take upon yourselves the task of seeing to it that their limpid light be not dimmed; and protect in their development those natural energies implanted in them by the guiding hand of God. ..."

Of the following day, the 6 May 1952, her son tells us:

"One day in May – the tulips were in full bloom – I sat with her over lunch at a window looking out on flowers and the sea, and told her about my meeting with a civil servant from Ghana, which was soon to gain its independence and was in urgent need of schools. He wanted to enlist the help of mother and myself for the training of teachers. 'If there are any children in need of help, then it is those poor children in the countries of Africa', mother said. 'Of course we must go'.

I asked her to think of the heat and the primitive conditions there. After all, she was eighty one.

'So then, you don't want me to come!' she said in mild reproach. 'Perhaps one day I shall go, and leave you here'.

THE ADVENTURE OF A LIFE IN THE SERVICE OF THE CHILD

'You will go nowhere where I cannot follow', I replied, remembering the way I used to boast as a child. Then I left the room to fetch an atlas with a map of Africa. When I returned, mother was dead. But she would have gone to Ghana – or to any other place in the world where children had need of her".

Maria Montessori is dead. But her spirit of love for children, of devotion to mankind, lives on. In Holland, the country that offered her such hospitality, there are today more than 160 Montessori Children's Houses or schools, and even several Montessori secondary schools. In Italy, her native land, hundreds of Montessori educational establishments have sprung up again, something that has also happened, since the late 1950s, in the USA. In India, countless Children's Houses use her methods. The International Montessori Association has been reestablished, with its headquarters in Amsterdam. There are branches of the Association in many countries. National and regional Montessori organizations, Montessori Children's Houses and schools are found nearly all over the world. These facts say something of the spirit of love and international reconciliation, something of the spirit of that humanity which this great Italian woman served throughout her life. It is particularly impressive that today Montessori's educational theory is held in high regard in those very countries which once had authoritarian or ideological regimes, such as Germany and Japan, and that clear signs of renewed interest are also coming from the former Communist countries of Central and Eastern Europe. After the horrors of the Second World War, Montessori, who had been proposed as a candidate for the Nobel Peace Prize in 1948, said:

"A man who boasts of his own superiority and that of his race never triumphs for very long. He falls, leaving murder and devastation behind him, as history repeatedly shows us. The truly great man is humble".

She was concerned with the child, whose task it is to construct the man of tomorrow, and not with gathering disciples around her, however many followers she may have acquired.

BASIC IDEAS OF MONTESSORI'S EDUCATIONAL THEORY

She had wanted to draw attention to the child, but people directed their gaze at her forefinger instead of at the child, she once said in her old age. And she nonchalantly added, in her own graphic manner, that this reminded her of the dog that, instead of going in the direction it had been shown, stared at the pointing finger and preferred to bite it rather than set off on the right path.

Let us try to comply with her wish and pay attention to the child, to the human beings that she loved with such devotion. In our era of uncertainty in education, it is on this basis that we should be concerned with Montessori's work, as we should be concerned with everything which is done with true devotion to the task of education. There is no other figure in the history of educational reform in the 20th century who has had such direct and indirect influence world-wide.

Bibliographical Appendix

Primary Literature
Used and recommended current publications

Aan de Basis van het Leven, Amsterdam 1951; [5]1996

The Absorbent Mind, Oxford 1988; cf. Aan de Basis van het Leven

The Advanced Montessori Method, Volume I, Oxford: Clio Press, 1991

The Advanced Montessori Method, Volume II, Oxford: Clio Press, 1995

I bambini viventi nella chiesa, Napoli 1922

The Child in the Church, London 1929, [2]1931

The Child in the Family, Oxford: Clio Press, 1989; cf. Das Kind in der Familie

The Child, Society and the World, Oxford: Clio Press, 1989

Citations in: What difference of age should there be among children in a Montessori-Group? by R. Joosten-Chotzen, in: Around the Child, Calcutta 1961 (Vol.VI, p.12–14)

The Discovery of the Child, Oxford: Clio Press, 1988

Door het Kind naar een Nieuwe Wereld, Heiloo 1941; Amsterdam [4]1996

To Educate the Human Potential, Oxford: Clio Press, 1989

Education and Peace, Oxford: Clio Press, 1992

Education For a New World, Oxford: Clio Press, 1989

The Formation of Man, Oxford: Clio Press, 1989

205

BASIC IDEAS OF MONTESSORI'S EDUCATIONAL THEORY

From Childhood to Adolescence, Oxford: Clio Press, 1994

Kinder, die in der Kirche leben, Freiburg 1964; cf. Gott und das Kind, Freiburg 1995

Grundlagen meiner Pädagogik, in: Handbuch der Erziehungs-wissenschaft, 3. Teil, Bd.1, München 1934, p. 265–285

Das Kind in der Familie, Stuttgart 1954, correct.ed. in: M. Montessori, Dem Leben helfen, Freiburg 1992, p. 9–73

Kinder sind anders, Stuttgart 1952

Mein Handbuch, Stuttgart 1922

La paix et l'éducation, Genève 1932

Pedagogical Anthropology, New York 1913

What You Should Know About Your Child, Oxford: Clio Press, 1989

Selected Secondary Literature

Böhm, Winfried, Maria Montessori, Hintergrund und Prinzipien ihres pädagogischen Denkens, Bad Heilbrunn 1969

Buytendijk, Frederik Jakobus Johannes, De zin van de vrij-heid in het menselijk bestaan, Utrecht/Antwerpen 1958

Calff, J.S., Van pionier tot mammoet. Het Amsterdams Montessori Lyceum 1930–1980, Amsterdam 1980

Hellbrügge, Theodor/Montessori, Mario M. sen. (Ed.): Die Montessori-Pädagogik und das behinderte Kind. Referate und Ergebnisse des 18. Internationalen Montessori-Kongresses, 4.-8. Juli 1977, München 1978

BIBLIOGRAPHICAL APPENDIX

Helming, Helene, Montessori-Pädagogik, Ein moderner Bildungsweg in konkreter Darstellung, Freiburg/Br. 1958, [14]1992

Holtstiege, Hildegard, Modell Montessori. Grundsätze und aktuelle Geltung der Montessori-Pädagogik, Freiburg [7]1994

Kramer, Rita, Maria Montessori. A Biography, New York 1976

Maccheroni, Anna, A True Romance, Edinburgh (1947)

– Come conobbi Maria Montessori, Rom 1956

MacCormick Rambusch, Nancy, Learning How to Learn. An American Approach to Montessori, Baltimore 1962

McVicker Hunt, J., Revisiting Montessori. In: Montessori, Maria, The Montessori Method; New York 1964; XI–XXXIX

Miller, Jean K., The Montessori Elementary School and Its Curriculum, Cleveland Oh. 1974

Montessori, Mario Dr., Montessori and her Work, Ass. Montessori Intern., (after 1936)

– Respect this House, in: The Mont. Magaz., Pilani 1949, p. 105–107

– Meine Mutter Maria Montessori, in: Read. Digest, Dt. Ausg. 10 (1965), p. 96–112

Montessori, Mario M., jun., Education for Human Development, New York 1977, Oxford: Clio Press, 1992

Moorman, Annemarie, Montessori concreet, Groningen 1979

207

BASIC IDEAS OF MONTESSORI'S EDUCATIONAL THEORY

Ochs, Elsa, Biographische Mitteilungen über Dr. Maria Montessori, in: Mont.-Nachrichten, Berlin, Aug. 1929

Orem, R.C., Montessori and the Special Child. An Application of Montessori Principles to Educating the Handicapped, the Disadvantaged and Other Children out of the Norm, New York 1970

Schulz-Benesch, Günter, Der Streit um Montessori, Freiburg 1961

– Montessori, Erträge der Forschung, Darmstadt 1980

Standing, Edwin Mortimer, Maria Montessori. Her Life and Work, London 1957

– The Montessori Revolution in Education, New York 1967

Some Bibliographies:

in: Böhm, Winfried, Bad Heilbrunn 1969 (145pp.)

Boehnlein, Mary Maher, The NAMTA Montessori Bibliography. A Bibliography of Source in the English Language, 1909–1984, Cleveland Heights, Ohio 1985, 209pp. (The North American Montessori Teachers' Association, The N.A.M.T.A. Quarterly, Vol. 10. No. 29)

Fleege, Virginia B., Montessori Index, Oak Park Illinois, [2]1974, 101pp.

Grazzini, Massimo, Bibliografia Montessori, Brescia 1965, 87pp.

Maiorca, Bruno, Bibliografia Montessori, in: I problemi della padagogia, Roma, 5/6 1972, p. 958–966; 4/5 1974, p. 754–764, 1 1976, p. 185–191

in: Schulz-Benesch, Günter, Der Streit um Montessori, Freiburg 1961 (159pp.)